Plan Pray Prosper™

WEEKLY PLANNER FOR THE WOMEN ON THE RISE

This Planner Belongs To:

_____

If Found Please Contact:

_____

This planner is for the person that is looking to manifest their goals through the power of prayer and planning.

Copyright © 2017 by Marsha Guerrier

Prayer Focus written by Maureen Smith

Scripture quotations are taken from the THE HOLY BIBLE, NEW INTERNATIONAL VERSION®, NIV® Copyright © 1973, 1978, 1984, 2011 by Biblica, Inc.® Used by permission. All rights reserved worldwide.

Women on the Rise NY, Inc. Publishing
P.O. Box 42
Valley Stream, NY 11582

Visit www.womenontheriseny.com

Blessings

For I know the plans I have for you," declares the Lord, "plans to prosper you and not to harm you, plans to give you hope and a future.

Jeremiah 29:11

There is surely a future hope for you,
and your hope will not be cut off.

Proverbs 23:18

He who was seated on the throne said, "I am making everything new! "Then he said, "Write this down, for these words are trustworthy and true."

Revelations 21:5

About the Planner

This planner is for the person that is seeking to manifest their goals through the power of prayer and planning. The Plan, Pray, Prosper Weekly Planner is a unique planner designed to help you plan your personal and professional life with intention and connect you closer to God through scripture. The planner is designed to empower you to create balance in your personal, family and professional life while you pursue your goals through weekly prayers and goals setting.

For years I've searched for a deeper spiritual connection with God and have always admired people that can recite scripture. The planner offers affirmations, monthly prayer focuses and weekly scriptures to help you focus and mediate on your goals. By meditating and memorizing the weekly scripture, you will be able to recite 52 scriptures to memory in one year.

I've included a SWOT Analysis (Strength, Weakness, Opportunity, Threats) to help you identify the internal and external factors within yourself and your life that can contribute to the success of you reaching your goals. Your internal factors are your Strengths and Weakness such as 'I'm a great organizer" and "I'm not so great at time management". Your external factors are the outside Opportunities and Threats such as "I will get three new clients this year through networking " and "There are several companies in my area selling similar products". Being aware of these factors will allow you to set goals that will utilize and avoid these factors that will directly impact the success of your goals.

It's the intention of Marsha Guerrier, the founder of Women on the Rise NY, Inc. along with her Spirtual Godmother, Maureen Smith to provide women a tool to assist them on their journey through goals setting and devotional prayer. We should seek God in everything we do on a daily basis. This planner will guide you towards praying with purpose and challenge you to study the Bible.

The beauty of Prayer is that it can happen anytime and anywhere, there is no wrong time to pray and vision the life you want. You've heard many people say that you should spend long periods of time praying and reading the Bible. If you have the time and can find the place to do so that is great, but for the women that are constantly on the go, I suggest you pray at any given moment, when you can. Remember God lives within you and will hear your prayers request.

As you work through the planner and identify your prayer request and goals, we do recommend that you read the monthly prayer focus along with the weekly scripture daily and allow yourself at least 10 minutes in that moment. It is important to be completely present and avoid any distractions while you plan and pray. When praying read aloud if you are in a private place with full authority and intention for the things that you want to manifest in my life. You will find that the words will breathe life into your soul, especially as you get further into your practice.

Be intentional and specific and watch your goals manifest the way God knows it can!

Blessings,
Marsha & Maureen

SWOT Analysis

STRENGTHS - identify your internal characteristics that will assist you in achieving your goals.

WEAKNESS - identify your internal characteristics that may prevent you from achieving your goals.

Use the SWOT Analysis to highlight internal and external factors that may help you in achieving your goals.

OPPORTUNITIES - identify the exterior factors that will assist you in achieving your goals.

THREATS - identify the exterior factors that will prevent you from achieving your goals.

Affirmations

I plan with courage and confidence.

—

I am a do-er. I take action and get things accomplished.

—

I release negativity. Instead I focus on positivity and productivity!

—

I am committed to being focused on my goals. I am worth it.

—

God is my Light and my Salvation.

—

I am created in the image of God, blessed with strength and wholeness.

—

Jesus give me Strength.

Affirmations

I relax, release any anxious thoughts, and peacefully rest in the presence of God.

———

God's love is working through me now and always.

———

I am ready to prosper beyond my wildest dreams.

———

I release all resistance to attracting prosperity.

———

I prosper in health. I prosper in finances. I prosper in love. I prosper in peace.

———

I surround myself with people who are likeminded and contribute to my abundance.

Year of _____ Prayer Focus

Season, what does this simple word conjure up in your mind? Are you picturing the bright sun shiny days of summer, the cool breezes of fall, winter snow flakes or the chill of plummeting temperatures or perhaps the new beginnings of a trees, flowers and plant life as spring emerges. These are all true and accurate scenarios, however there are other seasons. There are seasons of life, season, of time, in season (time or state of use), out of season (past it's usage time). Consider with me still other seasons, planting, reaping, prayer, fasting.

We are embarking on a new year, with plans for a new you, new adventures, new people, networks, ideas etc., and as we do let us see the year of 2018, (using a Webster's Dictionary definition), as a Season - a time to mature; in your dreams and aspirations, ripen, or condition by exposure to suitable conditions or treatment - with the truth of who God says you are, and what God says you can have.

We can tune in and activate this through faith, because God is not a liar and will do All that He said He will do, when we trust, believe and obey Him.

This is your Season and it is time to walk into your own by Faith, the waiting is over.

Why? Because You are more than conquerors in Christ Jesus.

Romans 8:31 What, then, shall we say in response to these things? If God is for us, who can be against us? Romans 8:37. No, in all these things we are more than conquerors through him who loved us.

Let's get ready to enter into the Favor and Promises of God for our families, our careers, our lives. Amen.

I pray that out of his glorious riches he may strengthen you with power through his Spirit in your inner being, so that Christ may dwell in your hearts through faith. And I pray that you, being rooted and established in love, may have power, together with all the Lord's holy people, to grasp how wide and long and high and deep is the love of Christ, and to know this love that surpasses knowledge—that you may be filled to the measure of all the fullness of God.

Ephesians 3:16-19

Prayer Request

PERSONAL REQUEST: _____

_____

_____

_____

_____

_____

FAMILY REQUEST: _____

_____

_____

_____

_____

_____

PROFESSIONAL REQUEST: _____

_____

_____

_____

_____

_____

_____

Praise the Lord, my soul, and forget not all his benefits - who forgives all your sins and heals all your diseases, who redeems your life from the pit and crowns you with love and compassion, who satisfies your desires with good things so that your youth is renewed like the eagle's.

Psalm 103:2-5

Month of _____

SUNDAY	MONDAY	TUESDAY
○	○	○
○	○	○
○	○	○
○	○	○
○	○	○

A Time for Everything

There is a time for everything, and a season for every activity under the heavens: a time to be born and a time to die, a time to plant and a time to uproot, a time to kill and a time to heal, a time to tear down and a time to build, a time to weep and a time to laugh, a time to mourn and a time to dance, a time to scatter stones and a time to gather them, a time to embrace and a time to refrain from embracing, a time to search and a time to give up, a time to keep and a time to throw away, a time to tear and a time to mend, a time to be silent and a time to speak, a time to love and a time to hate, a time for war and a time for peace.

Ecclesiastes 3:1-8

WEDNESDAY	THURSDAY	FRIDAY	SATURDAY
○	○	○	○
○	○	○	○
○	○	○	○
○	○	○	○
○	○	○	○

This month's goals: _____

_____

_____

_____

_____

_____

Heavenly Father, Creator of heaven and earth, author of time and seasons, I begin afresh this new year, expecting awesome new adventures as you teach me to discern the times. Father I submit myself to operate and carry out my daily activities in a manner that brings you glory and honor, because above all I want you to be pleased with my life and career. Your word says when I walk blameless you bless me. Psalm 119:1 Blessed are those whose ways are blameless, who walk according to the law of the Lord.

Teach me Lord how to respect and value time. Allow me to flow in the Spirit of your timing, that I not miss fantastic opportunities to see you move in my favor. I am open to allow you to teach me when to allow things, relationships or material things to die, when to move on. Teach me when to uproot, when to kill, to heal, to tear down, to build, to weep, laugh, to mourn and dance, and how to be mindful of others that may not understand where you are taking me and how you are taking me there. Please teach me to have patience with myself when I make mistakes and as grow in understanding your timing, my own time management and how I interact with others. I'm thrilled and welcome flourishing in maturing in this season.

I ask all of this in the matchless name of Jesus Christ. Amen

Prayer Request

_____
_____
_____
_____
_____
_____
_____
_____
_____
_____
_____
_____
_____
_____
_____

Monthly Reflection

What do you remember most about this month? Describe it.

_____

_____

_____

_____

_____

_____

Have you accomplished the goals you set forth this month, if not what changes would you make to accomplish your goals next month?

_____

_____

_____

_____

_____

How has the SWOT Analysis help you reach your goals?

_____

_____

_____

_____

_____

Month of _____

Faithful Words

SUNDAY	MONDAY	TUESDAY
○	○	○
○	○	○
○	○	○
○	○	○
○	○	○

The fundamental fact of existence is that this trust in God, this faith, is the firm foundation under everything that makes life worth living. It's our handle on what we can't see. The act of faith is what distinguished our ancestors, set them above the crowd. (The Message, MSG)

Hebrews 11:1-2

WEDNESDAY	THURSDAY	FRIDAY	SATURDAY
○	○	○	○
○	○	○	○
○	○	○	○
○	○	○	○
○	○	○	○

This month's goals: _____
_____
_____
_____
_____
_____

Prayer Focus

Faith means that I have acceptance, belief, surety, reliance and conviction of who you are and that your promises to me are indeed Yes and Amen (it is finished). Dare I not believe all that you say about me? You are God, my creator and and Jesus calls me friend, therefore I believe all that you say. I am indeed fearfully and wonderfully made (Psalm 139:14), and I am the head and not the tail, above and not beneath (Deut. 28:13). I can also rest assuredly that you have a plan and purpose for my life, and that it is a plan to prosper me, and not harm me, but give me a future (Jeremiah 29:11).

I therefore take you at your word faithful Father and I speak your words over me and my life. I give up negative speaking, and embrace and say what you say about me. You Father have said that the words that go out from your mouth will not return empty, but will accomplish what you desire and achieve the purpose for which you send it Isaiah 55:11 I therefore concede to your correction, and ask that by your Spirit teaching me, I quickly repent and change negative words into words of affirmation, and truth. You are such an awesome loving God, that wants only the best for me, and earnestly seek to be the best that you have for me. I have confidence that every issue that can arise in my life can be healed, or successful changed because I will not forfeit my blessings by not speaking and acting in faith according to your word. I will continually plant seeds of faith by speaking your truth, because it will reap a good harvest in due season.

Prayer Request

_____

_____

_____

_____

_____

_____

_____

_____

_____

_____

_____

_____

_____

_____

_____

Monthly Reflection

What do you remember most about this month? Describe it.

_____
_____
_____
_____
_____
_____
_____

Have you accomplished the goals you set forth this month, if not what changes would you make to accomplish your goals next month?

_____
_____
_____
_____
_____
_____

How has the SWOT Analysis help you reach your goals?

_____
_____
_____
_____
_____
_____
_____

Month of _____

SUNDAY	MONDAY	TUESDAY
○	○	○
○	○	○
○	○	○
○	○	○
○	○	○

Measuring and Maximizing

The Lord detests differing weights, and dishonest scales do not please him.

Proverbs 20:23

Jabez cried out to the God of Israel, "Oh, that you would bless me and enlarge my territory! Let your hand be with me, and keep me from harm so that I will be free from pain." And God granted his request.

1 Chronicles 4:10

WEDNESDAY	THURSDAY	FRIDAY	SATURDAY
○	○	○	○
○	○	○	○
○	○	○	○
○	○	○	○
○	○	○	○

This month's goals: _____
_____
_____
_____
_____
_____

Prayer Focus

Father in the name of Jesus let every day of my life be lived in honesty and truth, that the recompense for false and deceitful actions are not my reward. You are a God of truth, love and grace. Please allow those attributes to flow through me. There is always the temptation to seek, fame, fortune according to the pattern of the world. Never let me lose sight that my obedience to you and your pattern of life is counted as better than a sacrifice, and you reward those that follow your pattern of integrity.

Father I seek to maximize on your every promise for my life by being dutiful and faithful to what you have called me to do. Your word says ; "Whoever can be trusted with very little can also be trusted with much, and whoever is dishonest with very little will also be dishonest with much. Luke 16:10 I want to be found being honest in all things that your blessings will be bountiful and beyond what I thought possible. Embarking on this new month, allow me to connect with like minded people, make me aware of those that are not, and allow me to prosper as I offer my services to old as well as new prospective clients.

I love you and thank you Father for the abundance of promises to those that are faithful and true to your word. Words for me to live by, and for your glory. In Jesus Name I pray and say Amen.

Prayer Request

_____
_____
_____
_____
_____
_____
_____
_____
_____
_____
_____
_____
_____
_____

Monthly Reflection

What do you remember most about this month? Describe it.

_____

_____

_____

_____

_____

_____

Have you accomplished the goals you set forth this month, if not what changes would you make to accomplish your goals next month?

_____

_____

_____

_____

_____

_____

How has the SWOT Analysis help you reach your goals?

_____

_____

_____

_____

_____

_____

Month of _____

Ask, Seek, Knock for Assured Abundance

SUNDAY	MONDAY	TUESDAY
○	○	○
○	○	○
○	○	○
○	○	○
○	○	○

Ask and it will be given to you; seek and you will find; knock and the door will be opened to you. For everyone who asks receives; the one who seeks finds; and to the one who knocks, the door will be opened. "Which of you, if your son asks for bread, will give him a stone?

Matthew 7:7-12

WEDNESDAY	THURSDAY	FRIDAY	SATURDAY
○	○	○	○
○	○	○	○
○	○	○	○
○	○	○	○
○	○	○	○

This month's goals: _____

_____

_____

_____

_____

_____

Blessed Savior how wonderful are your ways. Your Holy book has endless accounts of the many people that came to you asking, seeking and knocking and you were ever so willing to meet them at their point of need. If I but sit and wonder about the man that could not enter the pool in time to be healed, yet when you saw him, you had compassion and healed him. Then the woman with the issue of blood, sick for over twelve years, she had only to seek to touch the hem of your clothing and gained her healing. What about the centurion whose daughter was sick, he asked that you just say "the word", and he had faith that his daughter would be healed and she was. There is nothing too hard for you Lord, nothing.

So I come in faith seeing the evidence of what you can do, asking that you meet my needs, as I continue on this journey of entrepreneurship. Allow me to know when to ask, and when to wait, when to seek opportunities or when to allow them to pass, and when to knock and which doors to pursue. Please Father give me favor with the people that I do business with; by orchestrating divine connections and networking. Allow me to be a blessing to others, as others bless me; grant cohesive collaborative projects to end with supernatural success. I'll never fail to give you the praise for all you do.

In Jesus name I pray and ask this and all things. Amen.

Prayer Request

_____

_____

_____

_____

_____

_____

_____

_____

_____

_____

_____

_____

_____

_____

Monthly Reflection

What do you remember most about this month? Describe it.

_____

_____

_____

_____

_____

_____

_____

Have you accomplished the goals you set forth this month, if not what changes would you make to accomplish your goals next month?

_____

_____

_____

_____

_____

_____

How has the SWOT Analysis help you reach your goals?

_____

_____

_____

_____

_____

_____

Month of _____

SUNDAY	MONDAY	TUESDAY
○	○	○
○	○	○
○	○	○
○	○	○
○	○	○

A Magnificent Milestones

I will remember the deeds of the Lord; yes, I will remember your miracles of long ago.

Psalm 77:11

[Generosity Encouraged] Remember this: Whoever sows sparingly will also reap sparingly, and whoever sows generously will also reap generously.

2 Corinthians 9:6

WEDNESDAY	THURSDAY	FRIDAY	SATURDAY
○	○	○	○
○	○	○	○
○	○	○	○
○	○	○	○
○	○	○	○

This month's goals: _____

_____

_____

_____

_____

_____

This is the day that the Lord has made, Let me/us be glad and rejoice in it.

Heavenly Father I will stop and take a close observance of where you have taken me from and where you have taken me to. I can only celebrate and praise you for all that you have done in and through me so far this year.

I will remember the doors opened the opportunities given, the successes won because I prepared, then exercised my faith to do all that you created me to do. I've worked on being fearless, because you say I am fearfully and wonderfully made and in your image.

Forgive me for the times that I did fear, or thought myself unworthy. Forgive me for worrying about how a bill would be paid or a deadline met, after I had sought your help through prayer and said I trusted you. I'm so grateful that you do not hold those things against me, but use them as opportunities to show me your love. Teachable moments that allow me to fall deeper in love with you, as I trust you more. May I share that compassion with others that they will mark the time they met me as a "milestone" in what you are doing in their lives.

May my milestones also be erected in new and creative ways as I help the poor, volunteer my time, taken and treasury to bless others as you have blessed me.

Prayer Request

_____
_____
_____
_____
_____
_____
_____
_____
_____
_____
_____
_____

Monthly Reflection

What do you remember most about this month? Describe it.

_____

_____

_____

_____

_____

_____

_____

Have you accomplished the goals you set forth this month, if not what changes would you make to accomplish your goals next month?

_____

_____

_____

_____

_____

_____

_____

How has the SWOT Analysis help you reach your goals?

_____

_____

_____

_____

_____

_____

_____

Month of _____

SUNDAY	MONDAY	TUESDAY
○	○	○
○	○	○
○	○	○
○	○	○
○	○	○

Be Joyful

Be joyful in hope, patient in affliction, faithful in prayer.

Romans 12:12

WEDNESDAY	THURSDAY	FRIDAY	SATURDAY
○	○	○	○
○	○	○	○
○	○	○	○
○	○	○	○
○	○	○	○

This month's goals: _____
_____
_____
_____
_____
_____

Prayer Focus

Father as I arrive at this mid-point of the year, I look back to assess the goals met, missed or changed. I also take time to examine the present and the future with joy. Did I miss a mark here and there? Yes I did, but those were teachable moments that have

granted me the opportunity to study and grasp new concepts and ideas. Nothing is wasted with you. Therefore I am joyful and rejoice in my craft because through it all I have accomplished much.

I can review the things that I could have done better and yet not punish myself for it, but rather plan with purpose and expectation and renewed hope. Your word says in Romans 5:5 And hope does not put us to shame, because God's love has been poured out into our hearts...

Reflecting on this allows me to know my work is not in vain. Indeed I press on toward the goal to win the prize for which God has called me... I will continue to patiently run this race, faithfully in prayer with good works.

Prayer Request

_____

_____

_____

_____

_____

_____

_____

_____

_____

_____

_____

_____

_____

_____

Monthly Reflection

What do you remember most about this month? Describe it.

_____

_____

_____

_____

_____

_____

_____

Have you accomplished the goals you set forth this month, if not what changes would you make to accomplish your goals next month?

_____

_____

_____

_____

_____

_____

How has the SWOT Analysis help you reach your goals?

_____

_____

_____

_____

_____

_____

Month of _____

SUNDAY	MONDAY	TUESDAY
○	○	○
○	○	○
○	○	○
○	○	○
○	○	○

Jubilee and Justice

Good will come to those who are generous and lend freely, who conduct their affairs with justice.

Psalm 112:5

WEDNESDAY	THURSDAY	FRIDAY	SATURDAY
○	○	○	○
○	○	○	○
○	○	○	○
○	○	○	○
○	○	○	○

This month's goals: _____
_____
_____
_____
_____
_____

Prayer Focus

Seven dear God is your perfect number of completion. On the seventh day God rested from His labor, after creating the heavens, earth and man.

During this time Father I pray that as I allow myself to take time to rest and marvel at your marvelous blessings; that the seeds planted throughout this year will continue to prosper and provide provisions for me. Please allow me this time to regroup, continuing to build my faith on the promises you have spoken over my life, business and career. I trust and therefore jubilantly, celebrate that every God ordained meeting, hiring opportunity, business connection will not be missed but only enhanced because you have allowed me to rest in you; because you care for me.

Prayer Request

_____
_____
_____
_____
_____
_____
_____
_____
_____
_____
_____
_____
_____
_____
_____
_____
_____

Monthly Reflection

What do you remember most about this month? Describe it.

_____
_____
_____
_____
_____
_____
_____

Have you accomplished the goals you set forth this month, if not what changes would you make to accomplish your goals next month?

_____
_____
_____
_____
_____
_____
_____

How has the SWOT Analysis help you reach your goals?

_____
_____
_____
_____
_____
_____
_____

Month of _____

New Aspirations

SUNDAY	MONDAY	TUESDAY
○	○	○
○	○	○
○	○	○
○	○	○
○	○	○

Blessed are those who find wisdom, those who gain understanding, for she is more profitable than silver and yields better returns than gold. She is more precious than rubies; nothing you desire can compare with her. Long life is in her right hand; in her left hand are riches and honor.

Proverbs 3:13-16

WEDNESDAY	THURSDAY	FRIDAY	SATURDAY
○	○	○	○
○	○	○	○
○	○	○	○
○	○	○	○
○	○	○	○

This month's goals: _____
_____
_____
_____
_____
_____

Prayer Focus

Father a new month, and new time to reflect and set new goals and aspirations for my life. I recognize and know that it is only through your wisdom and guidance will I succeed. So I sit in your magnificent presence and I sing songs of praise, as I find quiet, peace and safety, and ask that you give me Godly wisdom to accomplish all that you have prepared for me. I honor you God for all that you have done and will do for me.

I sit Lord with pen in hand, laptop ready, songs of praise in the background or in my heart. I am at the ready, excitedly waiting for you to download into my spirit the plans and purposes for this next season.

You do all things well, and exceedingly abundantly, above all I can ask or think, so I pray Father that you make clear the plans as I record them, so that I don't miss one detail. I always want you to be proud of me, as I help others know that it is only through you that I have succeeded.

Prayer Request

_____

_____

_____

_____

_____

_____

_____

_____

_____

_____

_____

_____

_____

_____

Monthly Reflection

What do you remember most about this month? Describe it.

_____
_____
_____
_____
_____
_____
_____
_____

Have you accomplished the goals you set forth this month, if not what changes would you make to accomplish your goals next month?

_____
_____
_____
_____
_____
_____
_____

How has the SWOT Analysis help you reach your goals?

_____
_____
_____
_____
_____
_____

Month of _____

SUNDAY	MONDAY	TUESDAY
○	○	○
○	○	○
○	○	○
○	○	○
○	○	○

Specifications

She is like the merchant ships, bringing her food from afar. She gets up while it is still night; she provides food for her family and portions for her female servants. She considers a field and buys it; out of her earnings she plants a vineyard.

Proverbs 31:14-16

WEDNESDAY	THURSDAY	FRIDAY	SATURDAY
○	○	○	○
○	○	○	○
○	○	○	○
○	○	○	○
○	○	○	○

This month's goals: _____
_____
_____
_____
_____
_____

Prayer Focus

Heavenly Father how comforting it is to know how much you love your daughters. You have made us beautiful in your sight, and you call us daughters of the Most High. Thank you Lord, and thank you for giving me/us the wisdom and knack for being women of worth, women of business, women after your own heart. You thought so highly of our ability that memorialized us in Proverbs 31. I'm ecstatic that you see me in that light. I so want to fulfill and possess the characteristics of the Proverbs 31 woman, that I implore you to direct my footsteps that I might study to show myself approved, embracing those attributes and living out that lifestyle.

Prayer Request

_____

_____

_____

_____

_____

_____

_____

_____

_____

_____

_____

_____

_____

_____

_____

_____

Monthly Reflection

What do you remember most about this month? Describe it.

_____
_____
_____
_____
_____
_____
_____

Have you accomplished the goals you set forth this month, if not what changes would you make to accomplish your goals next month?

_____
_____
_____
_____
_____
_____

How has the SWOT Analysis help you reach your goals?

_____
_____
_____
_____
_____
_____
_____

Month of _____

Opportunities and Occasions

SUNDAY	MONDAY	TUESDAY
○	○	○
○	○	○
○	○	○
○	○	○
○	○	○

Now he who supplies seed to the sower and bread for food will also supply and increase your store of seed and will enlarge the harvest of your righteousness. You will be enriched in every way so that you can be generous on every occasion, and through us your generosity will result in thanksgiving to God. This service that you perform is not only supplying the needs of the Lord's people but is also overflowing in many expressions of thanks to God.

2 Corinthians 9:10-12

WEDNESDAY	THURSDAY	FRIDAY	SATURDAY
○	○	○	○
○	○	○	○
○	○	○	○
○	○	○	○
○	○	○	○

This month's goals: _____

_____

_____

_____

_____

_____

Prayer Focus

Oh God, how excellent are your ways. You give me seeds to sow, bread for food and more than enough to increase my storage supply. There is no God better than you Lord, and because you have been so good to me. You continue to make me to thrive throughout this year. You've increase my faith, given me a harvest, allowed me to rest and provided additional plans and aspirations for my future. Lord let my compassion be that of a grateful heart. Just as I have planned and purposed how to achieve career goals, allow me to plan and purpose to give to those less fortunate than myself, that they too will know that you love them.

Allow me to seek opportunities and occasions to be a blessing to others as I demonstrate my gratitude and acts of thanksgiving to you.

Prayer Request

_____
_____
_____
_____
_____
_____
_____
_____
_____
_____
_____
_____
_____
_____
_____
_____

Monthly Reflection

What do you remember most about this month? Describe it.

_____
_____
_____
_____
_____
_____

Have you accomplished the goals you set forth this month, if not what changes would you make to accomplish your goals next month?

_____
_____
_____
_____
_____
_____

How has the SWOT Analysis help you reach your goals?

_____
_____
_____
_____
_____
_____

Month of _____

Notable Thanksgiving

SUNDAY	MONDAY	TUESDAY
○	○	○
○	○	○
○	○	○
○	○	○
○	○	○

Know that the Lord is God. It is he who made us, and we are his[a]; we are his people, the sheep of his pasture. Enter his gates with thanksgiving and his courts with praise; give thanks to him and praise his name. For the Lord is good and his love endures forever; his faithfulness continues through all generations.

Psalm 100:3-5

WEDNESDAY	THURSDAY	FRIDAY	SATURDAY
○	○	○	○
○	○	○	○
○	○	○	○
○	○	○	○
○	○	○	○

This month's goals: _____

_____
_____
_____
_____
_____

Prayer Focus

It is said that Hallelujah is the highest praise. I sing Hallelujah to the King of Kings and the Lord of Lords. My soul reflects on your goodness and promises fulfilled. I can only overflow with THANKSGIVING!

You are and have been my rock and my fortress. It is in you I place my trust, and will therefore requesting nothing from you this month (fasting from asking), only using my prayer time to Praise, Worship and Thank you for your (too many to number) acts of goodness, and mercy towards me.

Prayer Request

_____
_____
_____
_____
_____
_____
_____
_____
_____
_____
_____
_____
_____
_____
_____
_____
_____

Monthly Reflection

What do you remember most about this month? Describe it.

_____
_____
_____
_____
_____
_____
_____

Have you accomplished the goals you set forth this month, if not what changes would you make to accomplish your goals next month?

_____
_____
_____
_____
_____
_____
_____

How has the SWOT Analysis help you reach your goals?

_____
_____
_____
_____
_____
_____
_____

Month of _____

SUNDAY	MONDAY	TUESDAY
○	○	○
○	○	○
○	○	○
○	○	○
○	○	○

Dedicated and Devoted

Therefore, I urge you, brothers and sisters, in view of God's mercy, to offer your bodies as a living sacrifice, holy and pleasing to God—this is your true and proper worship.

Romans 12:1

WEDNESDAY	THURSDAY	FRIDAY	SATURDAY
○	○	○	○
○	○	○	○
○	○	○	○
○	○	○	○
○	○	○	○

This month's goals: _____
_____
_____
_____
_____
_____

Prayer Focus

Father as we come to the end of yet a marvelous year I want to scream from the rooftops how awesome is my God. You have taken me from glory to glory, as I have immersed myself into believing, speaking and acting in faith on your word.

You have taught me to discern the times, not fear, but pray and see your marvelous works unfold. You've taught me to plan, plant, water and expect a harvest because I seek to be good and righteous. You've allowed me to volunteer time and talents into the lives of others, because of your great favor towards me. I've been shown the need for rest and refreshing, given me new aspirations and occasions to serve with thanksgiving.

I so love my time spent with you, am overwhelmed by the work, fun and success of this year of new adventures. It's you I love and wholly devote myself to living life according to your plan and purpose for my life.

Prayer Request

_____

_____

_____

_____

_____

_____

_____

_____

_____

_____

_____

_____

_____

_____

Monthly Reflection

What do you remember most about this month? Describe it.

_____
_____
_____
_____
_____
_____
_____

Have you accomplished the goals you set forth this month, if not what changes would you make to accomplish your goals next month?

_____
_____
_____
_____
_____
_____

How has the SWOT Analysis help you reach your goals?

_____
_____
_____
_____
_____
_____
_____

Notes to Self

Notes to Self

Week of _____

Behold, I am doing a new thing; now it springs forth, do you not perceive it? I will make a way in the wilderness and rivers in the desert.

Isaiah 43:19

Prayer Request

PERSONAL REQUEST: _____

FAMILY REQUEST: _____

PROFESSIONAL REQUEST: _____

Goals

PERSONAL GOALS: _____

_____

_____

_____

_____

_____

_____

_____

FAMILY GOALS: _____

_____

_____

_____

_____

_____

PROFESSIONAL GOALS: _____

_____

_____

_____

_____

_____

Important Dates:

Event Name_____

Date_____

Event Name_____

Date_____

Event Name_____

Date_____

Mind and Body

- Do remember to call someone you love.
- Do remember to exercise your mind and body.
- Do remember to drink plenty of water
- Do remember to get plenty of rest.

/ Week of _____

	Monday	Tuesday	Wednesday
5 am			
6 am			
7 am			
8 am			
9 am			
10 am			
11 am			
12 pm			
1 pm			
2 pm			
3 pm			
4 pm			
5 pm			
6 pm			
7 pm			
8 pm			
9 pm			
10 pm			
	Water ○○○○○○○○	Water ○○○○○○○○	Water ○○○○○○○○

	Thursday	Friday		Saturday
5 am			9 am	
6 am			10 am	
7 am			11 am	
8 am			12 pm	
9 am			1 pm	
10 am			2 pm	
11 am			3 pm	
12 pm			4 pm	
1 pm				Water ◊◊◊◊◊◊◊◊
2 pm				Sunday
3 pm			9 am	
4 pm			10 am	
5 pm			11 am	
6 pm			12 pm	
7 pm			1 pm	
8 pm			2 pm	
9 pm			3 pm	
10 pm			4 pm	
	Water ◊◊◊◊◊◊◊◊	Water ◊◊◊◊◊◊◊◊		Water ◊◊◊◊◊◊◊

Week of _____

The steadfast love of the Lord never ceases; his mercies never come to an end; they are new every morning; great is your faithfulness. "The Lord is my portion," says my soul, "therefore I will hope in him."

Lamentations 3:22-24

Prayer Request

PERSONAL REQUEST: _____

_____

_____

_____

_____

FAMILY REQUEST: _____

_____

_____

_____

_____

_____

PROFESSIONAL REQUEST: _____

_____

_____

_____

_____

_____

_____

_____

Goals

PERSONAL GOALS: _____

_____
_____
_____
_____
_____
_____
_____

FAMILY GOALS: _____

_____
_____
_____
_____
_____
_____
_____

PROFESSIONAL GOALS: _____

_____
_____
_____
_____
_____
_____

Important Dates:

Event Name_____

Date_____

Event Name_____

Date_____

Event Name_____

Date_____

Mind and Body

- Do remember to call someone you love.
- Do remember to exercise your mind and body.
- Do remember to drink plenty of water
- Do remember to get plenty of rest.

Week of _____

	Monday	Tuesday	Wednesday
5 am			
6 am			
7 am			
8 am			
9 am			
10 am			
11 am			
12 pm			
1 pm			
2 pm			
3 pm			
4 pm			
5 pm			
6 pm			
7 pm			
8 pm			
9 pm			
10 pm			
	Water ὁ ὁ ὁ ὁ ὁ ὁ ὁ ὁ	Water ὁ ὁ ὁ ὁ ὁ ὁ ὁ ὁ	Water ὁ ὁ ὁ ὁ ὁ ὁ ὁ ὁ

	Thursday	Friday		Saturday
5 am			9 am	
6 am			10 am	
7 am			11 am	
8 am			12 pm	
9 am			1 pm	
10 am			2 pm	
11 am			3 pm	
12 pm			4 pm	
1 pm				Water 💧💧💧💧💧💧💧
2 pm				Sunday
3 pm			9 am	
4 pm			10 am	
5 pm			11 am	
6 pm			12 pm	
7 pm			1 pm	
8 pm			2 pm	
9 pm			3 pm	
10 pm			4 pm	
	Water 💧💧💧💧💧💧💧	Water 💧💧💧💧💧💧💧		Water 💧💧💧💧💧💧💧

Week of _____

He will wipe away every tear from their eyes, and death shall be no more, neither shall there be mourning, nor crying, nor pain anymore, for the former things have passed away."

Revelation 21:4

Prayer Request

PERSONAL REQUEST: _____

_____

_____

_____

_____

FAMILY REQUEST: _____

_____

_____

_____

_____

_____

PROFESSIONAL REQUEST: _____

_____

_____

_____

_____

_____

_____

_____

Goals

PERSONAL GOALS: _____
_____
_____
_____
_____
_____
_____

FAMILY GOALS: _____
_____
_____
_____
_____
_____

PROFESSIONAL GOALS: _____
_____
_____
_____
_____
_____

Important Dates:

Event Name_____
Date_____
Event Name_____
Date_____
Event Name_____
Date_____

Mind and Body

- Do remember to call someone you love.
- Do remember to exercise your mind and body.
- Do remember to drink plenty of water
- Do remember to get plenty of rest.

Week of _____

	Monday	Tuesday	Wednesday
5 am			
6 am			
7 am			
8 am			
9 am			
10 am			
11 am			
12 pm			
1 pm			
2 pm			
3 pm			
4 pm			
5 pm			
6 pm			
7 pm			
8 pm			
9 pm			
10 pm			
	Water ⬦⬦⬦⬦⬦⬦⬦⬦	Water ⬦⬦⬦⬦⬦⬦⬦⬦	Water ⬦⬦⬦⬦⬦⬦⬦⬦

	Thursday	Friday		Saturday
5 am			9 am	
6 am			10 am	
7 am			11 am	
8 am			12 pm	
9 am			1 pm	
10 am			2 pm	
11 am			3 pm	
12 pm			4 pm	
1 pm				Water 💧💧💧💧💧💧💧
2 pm				Sunday
3 pm			9 am	
4 pm			10 am	
5 pm			11 am	
6 pm			12 pm	
7 pm			1 pm	
8 pm			2 pm	
9 pm			3 pm	
10 pm			4 pm	
	Water 💧💧💧💧💧💧💧💧	Water 💧💧💧💧💧💧💧		Water 💧💧💧💧💧💧💧

Week of _____

Therefore I tell you, her sins, which are many, are forgiven—for she loved much. But he who is forgiven little, loves little."

Luke 7:47

Prayer Request

PERSONAL REQUEST: _____

_____

_____

_____

_____

FAMILY REQUEST: _____

_____

_____

_____

_____

_____

PROFESSIONAL REQUEST: _____

_____

_____

_____

_____

_____

_____

Goals

PERSONAL GOALS: _____

_____

_____

_____

_____

_____

_____

FAMILY GOALS: _____

_____

_____

_____

_____

_____

PROFESSIONAL GOALS: _____

_____

_____

_____

_____

_____

Important Dates:

Event Name_____

Date_____

Event Name_____

Date_____

Event Name_____

Date_____

Mind and Body

- Do remember to call someone you love.
- Do remember to exercise your mind and body.
- Do remember to drink plenty of water
- Do remember to get plenty of rest.

Week of _____

	Monday	Tuesday	Wednesday
5 am			
6 am			
7 am			
8 am			
9 am			
10 am			
11 am			
12 pm			
1 pm			
2 pm			
3 pm			
4 pm			
5 pm			
6 pm			
7 pm			
8 pm			
9 pm			
10 pm			
	Water 💧💧💧💧💧💧💧💧	Water 💧💧💧💧💧💧💧💧	Water 💧💧💧💧💧💧💧💧

	Thursday	Friday		Saturday
5 am			9 am	
6 am			10 am	
7 am			11 am	
8 am			12 pm	
9 am			1 pm	
10 am			2 pm	
11 am			3 pm	
12 pm			4 pm	
1 pm				Water 💧💧💧💧💧💧💧💧
2 pm				Sunday
3 pm			9 am	
4 pm			10 am	
5 pm			11 am	
6 pm			12 pm	
7 pm			1 pm	
8 pm			2 pm	
9 pm			3 pm	
10 pm			4 pm	
	Water 💧💧💧💧💧💧💧💧	Water 💧💧💧💧💧💧💧💧		Water 💧💧💧💧💧💧💧💧

Week of _____

But they who wait for the Lord shall renew their strength; they shall mount up with wings like eagles; they shall run and not be weary; they shall walk and not faint.

Isaiah 40:31

Prayer Request

PERSONAL REQUEST: _____
_____
_____
_____
_____

FAMILY REQUEST: _____
_____
_____
_____
_____

PROFESSIONAL REQUEST: _____
_____
_____
_____
_____
_____
_____

Goals

PERSONAL GOALS: _____

_____

_____

_____

_____

_____

_____

FAMILY GOALS: _____

_____

_____

_____

_____

_____

PROFESSIONAL GOALS: _____

_____

_____

_____

_____

_____

Important Dates:

Event Name_____

Date_____

Event Name_____

Date_____

Event Name_____

Date_____

Mind and Body

- Do remember to call someone you love.
- Do remember to exercise your mind and body.
- Do remember to drink plenty of water
- Do remember to get plenty of rest.

Week of _____

	Monday	Tuesday	Wednesday
5 am			
6 am			
7 am			
8 am			
9 am			
10 am			
11 am			
12 pm			
1 pm			
2 pm			
3 pm			
4 pm			
5 pm			
6 pm			
7 pm			
8 pm			
9 pm			
10 pm			
	Water ◊◊◊◊◊◊◊◊	Water ◊◊◊◊◊◊◊◊	Water ◊◊◊◊◊◊◊◊

	Thursday	Friday		Saturday
5 am			9 am	
6 am			10 am	
7 am			11 am	
8 am			12 pm	
9 am			1 pm	
10 am			2 pm	
11 am			3 pm	
12 pm			4 pm	
1 pm				Water 〇〇〇〇〇〇〇〇
2 pm				Sunday
3 pm			9 am	
4 pm			10 am	
5 pm			11 am	
6 pm			12 pm	
7 pm			1 pm	
8 pm			2 pm	
9 pm			3 pm	
10 pm			4 pm	
	Water 〇〇〇〇〇〇〇〇	Water 〇〇〇〇〇〇〇〇		Water 〇〇〇〇〇〇〇〇

Week of _____

"Ask, and it will be given to you; seek, and you will find; knock, and it will be opened to you.

Matthew 7:7

Prayer Request

PERSONAL REQUEST: _____
_____
_____
_____
_____

FAMILY REQUEST: _____
_____
_____
_____
_____

PROFESSIONAL REQUEST: _____
_____
_____
_____
_____
_____

Goals

PERSONAL GOALS: _____

_____

_____

_____

_____

_____

_____

FAMILY GOALS: _____

_____

_____

_____

_____

_____

PROFESSIONAL GOALS: _____

_____

_____

_____

_____

_____

Important Dates:

Event Name_____

Date_____

Event Name_____

Date_____

Event Name_____

Date_____

Mind and Body

- Do remember to call someone you love.
- Do remember to exercise your mind and body.
- Do remember to drink plenty of water
- Do remember to get plenty of rest.

Week of _____

	Monday	Tuesday	Wednesday
5 am			
6 am			
7 am			
8 am			
9 am			
10 am			
11 am			
12 pm			
1 pm			
2 pm			
3 pm			
4 pm			
5 pm			
6 pm			
7 pm			
8 pm			
9 pm			
10 pm			
	Water ◊◊◊◊◊◊◊◊	Water ◊◊◊◊◊◊◊◊	Water ◊◊◊◊◊◊◊◊

	Thursday	Friday		Saturday
5 am			9 am	
6 am			10 am	
7 am			11 am	
8 am			12 pm	
9 am			1 pm	
10 am			2 pm	
11 am			3 pm	
12 pm			4 pm	
1 pm				Water ◊◊◊◊◊◊◊◊
2 pm				Sunday
3 pm			9 am	
4 pm			10 am	
5 pm			11 am	
6 pm			12 pm	
7 pm			1 pm	
8 pm			2 pm	
9 pm			3 pm	
10 pm			4 pm	
	Water ◊◊◊◊◊◊◊◊	Water ◊◊◊◊◊◊◊◊		Water ◊◊◊◊◊◊◊◊

Week of _____

If my people who are called by my name humble themselves, and pray and seek my face and turn from their wicked ways, then I will hear from heaven and will forgive their sin and heal their land.

2 Chronicles 7:14

Prayer Request

PERSONAL REQUEST: _____

_____

_____

_____

_____

FAMILY REQUEST: _____

_____

_____

_____

_____

_____

PROFESSIONAL REQUEST: _____

_____

_____

_____

_____

_____

_____

Goals

PERSONAL GOALS: _____

_____

_____

_____

_____

_____

_____

_____

FAMILY GOALS: _____

_____

_____

_____

_____

_____

_____

PROFESSIONAL GOALS: _____

_____

_____

_____

_____

_____

_____

Important Dates:

Event Name_____

Date_____

Event Name_____

Date_____

Event Name_____

Date_____

Mind and Body

- Do remember to call someone you love.
- Do remember to exercise your mind and body.
- Do remember to drink plenty of water
- Do remember to get plenty of rest.

Week of _____

	Monday	Tuesday	Wednesday
5 am			
6 am			
7 am			
8 am			
9 am			
10 am			
11 am			
12 pm			
1 pm			
2 pm			
3 pm			
4 pm			
5 pm			
6 pm			
7 pm			
8 pm			
9 pm			
10 pm			
	Water ◊◊◊◊◊◊◊◊	Water ◊◊◊◊◊◊◊◊	Water ◊◊◊◊◊◊◊◊

	Thursday	Friday		Saturday
5 am			9 am	
6 am			10 am	
7 am			11 am	
8 am			12 pm	
9 am			1 pm	
10 am			2 pm	
11 am			3 pm	
12 pm			4 pm	
1 pm				Water 💧💧💧💧💧💧💧
2 pm				**Sunday**
3 pm			9 am	
4 pm			10 am	
5 pm			11 am	
6 pm			12 pm	
7 pm			1 pm	
8 pm			2 pm	
9 pm			3 pm	
10 pm			4 pm	
	Water 💧💧💧💧💧💧💧	Water 💧💧💧💧💧💧💧		Water 💧💧💧💧💧💧💧

Week of _____

"So keep the words of this covenant to do them, that you may prosper in all that you do.

Deuteronomy 29:9

Prayer Request

PERSONAL REQUEST: _____

_____
_____
_____
_____

FAMILY REQUEST: _____

_____
_____
_____
_____
_____

PROFESSIONAL REQUEST: _____

_____
_____
_____
_____
_____
_____

Goals

PERSONAL GOALS: _____

_____
_____
_____
_____
_____
_____
_____

FAMILY GOALS: _____

_____
_____
_____
_____
_____
_____

PROFESSIONAL GOALS: _____

_____
_____
_____
_____
_____
_____

Important Dates:

Event Name_____
Date_____
Event Name_____
Date_____
Event Name_____
Date_____

Mind and Body

- Do remember to call someone you love.
- Do remember to exercise your mind and body.
- Do remember to drink plenty of water
- Do remember to get plenty of rest.

Week of _____

	Monday	Tuesday	Wednesday
5 am			
6 am			
7 am			
8 am			
9 am			
10 am			
11 am			
12 pm			
1 pm			
2 pm			
3 pm			
4 pm			
5 pm			
6 pm			
7 pm			
8 pm			
9 pm			
10 pm			
	Water ⬥⬥⬥⬥⬥⬥⬥⬥	Water ⬥⬥⬥⬥⬥⬥⬥⬥	Water ⬥⬥⬥⬥⬥⬥⬥⬥

	Thursday	Friday		Saturday
5 am			9 am	
6 am			10 am	
7 am			11 am	
8 am			12 pm	
9 am			1 pm	
10 am			2 pm	
11 am			3 pm	
12 pm			4 pm	
1 pm				Water 💧💧💧💧💧💧💧
2 pm				**Sunday**
3 pm			9 am	
4 pm			10 am	
5 pm			11 am	
6 pm			12 pm	
7 pm			1 pm	
8 pm			2 pm	
9 pm			3 pm	
10 pm			4 pm	
	Water 💧💧💧💧💧💧💧	Water 💧💧💧💧💧💧💧		Water 💧💧💧💧💧💧💧

Week of _____

Therefore let him who thinks he stands take heed that he does not fall. No temptation has overtaken you but such as is common to man; and God is faithful, who will not allow you to be tempted beyond what you are able, but with the temptation will provide the way of escape also, so that you will be able to endure it.

1 Corinthians 10:12-13

Prayer Request

PERSONAL REQUEST: _____

_____

_____

_____

_____

FAMILY REQUEST: _____

_____

_____

_____

_____

_____

PROFESSIONAL REQUEST: _____

_____

_____

_____

_____

_____

_____

Goals

PERSONAL GOALS: _____

_____
_____
_____
_____
_____
_____
_____

FAMILY GOALS: _____

_____
_____
_____
_____
_____
_____

PROFESSIONAL GOALS: _____

_____
_____
_____
_____
_____
_____

Important Dates:

Event Name_____

Date_____

Event Name_____

Date_____

Event Name_____

Date_____

Mind and Body

- Do remember to call someone you love.
- Do remember to exercise your mind and body.
- Do remember to drink plenty of water
- Do remember to get plenty of rest.

Week of _____

	Monday	Tuesday	Wednesday
5 am			
6 am			
7 am			
8 am			
9 am			
10 am			
11 am			
12 pm			
1 pm			
2 pm			
3 pm			
4 pm			
5 pm			
6 pm			
7 pm			
8 pm			
9 pm			
10 pm			
	Water ߋߋߋߋߋߋߋߋ	Water ߋߋߋߋߋߋߋߋ	Water ߋߋߋߋߋߋߋߋ

	Thursday	Friday		Saturday
5 am			9 am	
6 am			10 am	
7 am			11 am	
8 am			12 pm	
9 am			1 pm	
10 am			2 pm	
11 am			3 pm	
12 pm			4 pm	
1 pm				Water 💧💧💧💧💧💧💧💧
2 pm				Sunday
3 pm			9 am	
4 pm			10 am	
5 pm			11 am	
6 pm			12 pm	
7 pm			1 pm	
8 pm			2 pm	
9 pm			3 pm	
10 pm			4 pm	
	Water 💧💧💧💧💧💧💧💧	Water 💧💧💧💧💧💧💧💧		Water 💧💧💧💧💧💧💧💧

Week of _____

A just balance and scales belong to the LORD; All the weights of the bag are His concern.

Proverbs 16:11

Prayer Request

PERSONAL REQUEST: _____

_____

_____

_____

_____

FAMILY REQUEST: _____

_____

_____

_____

_____

_____

PROFESSIONAL REQUEST: _____

_____

_____

_____

_____

_____

_____

Goals

PERSONAL GOALS: _____

_____

_____

_____

_____

_____

_____

FAMILY GOALS: _____

_____

_____

_____

_____

_____

PROFESSIONAL GOALS: _____

_____

_____

_____

_____

_____

Important Dates:

Event Name_____

Date_____

Event Name_____

Date_____

Event Name_____

Date_____

Mind and Body

- Do remember to call someone you love.
- Do remember to exercise your mind and body.
- Do remember to drink plenty of water
- Do remember to get plenty of rest.

Week of _____

	Monday	Tuesday	Wednesday
5 am			
6 am			
7 am			
8 am			
9 am			
10 am			
11 am			
12 pm			
1 pm			
2 pm			
3 pm			
4 pm			
5 pm			
6 pm			
7 pm			
8 pm			
9 pm			
10 pm			
	Water ◊◊◊◊◊◊◊◊	Water ◊◊◊◊◊◊◊◊	Water ◊◊◊◊◊◊◊◊

	Thursday	Friday		Saturday
5 am			9 am	
6 am			10 am	
7 am			11 am	
8 am			12 pm	
9 am			1 pm	
10 am			2 pm	
11 am			3 pm	
12 pm			4 pm	
1 pm				Water 🌢🌢🌢🌢🌢🌢🌢
2 pm				Sunday
3 pm			9 am	
4 pm			10 am	
5 pm			11 am	
6 pm			12 pm	
7 pm			1 pm	
8 pm			2 pm	
9 pm			3 pm	
10 pm			4 pm	
	Water 🌢🌢🌢🌢🌢🌢🌢	Water 🌢🌢🌢🌢🌢🌢🌢		Water 🌢🌢🌢🌢🌢🌢🌢

Week of _____

Therefore, my beloved brethren, be steadfast, immovable, always abounding in the work of the Lord, knowing that your toil is not in vain in the Lord.

1 Corinthians 15:58

Prayer Request

PERSONAL REQUEST: _____

_____

_____

_____

_____

FAMILY REQUEST: _____

_____

_____

_____

_____

_____

PROFESSIONAL REQUEST: _____

_____

_____

_____

_____

_____

_____

Goals

PERSONAL GOALS: _____

_____

_____

_____

_____

_____

_____

_____

FAMILY GOALS: _____

_____

_____

_____

_____

_____

_____

PROFESSIONAL GOALS: _____

_____

_____

_____

_____

_____

_____

Important Dates:

Event Name_____

Date_____

Event Name_____

Date_____

Event Name_____

Date_____

Mind and Body

- Do remember to call someone you love.
- Do remember to exercise your mind and body.
- Do remember to drink plenty of water
- Do remember to get plenty of rest.

Week of _____

	Monday	Tuesday	Wednesday
5 am			
6 am			
7 am			
8 am			
9 am			
10 am			
11 am			
12 pm			
1 pm			
2 pm			
3 pm			
4 pm			
5 pm			
6 pm			
7 pm			
8 pm			
9 pm			
10 pm			
	Water ⬦⬦⬦⬦⬦⬦⬦⬦	Water ⬦⬦⬦⬦⬦⬦⬦⬦	Water ⬦⬦⬦⬦⬦⬦⬦⬦

	Thursday	Friday		Saturday
5 am			9 am	
6 am			10 am	
7 am			11 am	
8 am			12 pm	
9 am			1 pm	
10 am			2 pm	
11 am			3 pm	
12 pm			4 pm	
1 pm				Water 💧💧💧💧💧💧💧💧
2 pm				Sunday
3 pm			9 am	
4 pm			10 am	
5 pm			11 am	
6 pm			12 pm	
7 pm			1 pm	
8 pm			2 pm	
9 pm			3 pm	
10 pm			4 pm	
	Water 💧💧💧💧💧💧💧💧	Water 💧💧💧💧💧💧💧💧		Water 💧💧💧💧💧💧💧💧

Week of _____

Trust in the LORD with all your heart And do not lean on your own understanding. In all your ways acknowledge Him, And He will make your paths straight.

Proverbs 3:5-6

Prayer Request

PERSONAL REQUEST: _____

_____

_____

_____

_____

FAMILY REQUEST: _____

_____

_____

_____

_____

_____

PROFESSIONAL REQUEST: _____

_____

_____

_____

_____

_____

_____

Goals

PERSONAL GOALS: _____

_____

_____

_____

_____

_____

_____

FAMILY GOALS: _____

_____

_____

_____

_____

_____

PROFESSIONAL GOALS: _____

_____

_____

_____

_____

_____

Important Dates:

Event Name_____

Date_____

Event Name_____

Date_____

Event Name_____

Date_____

Mind and Body

- Do remember to call someone you love.
- Do remember to exercise your mind and body.
- Do remember to drink plenty of water
- Do remember to get plenty of rest.

Week of _____

	Monday	Tuesday	Wednesday
5 am			
6 am			
7 am			
8 am			
9 am			
10 am			
11 am			
12 pm			
1 pm			
2 pm			
3 pm			
4 pm			
5 pm			
6 pm			
7 pm			
8 pm			
9 pm			
10 pm			
	Water ○○○○○○○○	Water ○○○○○○○○	Water ○○○○○○○○

	Thursday	Friday		Saturday
5 am			9 am	
6 am			10 am	
7 am			11 am	
8 am			12 pm	
9 am			1 pm	
10 am			2 pm	
11 am			3 pm	
12 pm			4 pm	
1 pm				Water 💧💧💧💧💧💧💧
2 pm				**Sunday**
3 pm			9 am	
4 pm			10 am	
5 pm			11 am	
6 pm			12 pm	
7 pm			1 pm	
8 pm			2 pm	
9 pm			3 pm	
10 pm			4 pm	
	Water 💧💧💧💧💧💧💧	Water 💧💧💧💧💧💧💧		Water 💧💧💧💧💧💧💧

Week of _____

You crown the year with your bounty, and your carts overflow with abundance.

Psalm 65:11

Prayer Request

PERSONAL REQUEST: _____

_____

_____

_____

_____

FAMILY REQUEST: _____

_____

_____

_____

_____

_____

PROFESSIONAL REQUEST: _____

_____

_____

_____

_____

_____

_____

Goals

PERSONAL GOALS: _____

_____

_____

_____

_____

_____

_____

FAMILY GOALS: _____

_____

_____

_____

_____

_____

PROFESSIONAL GOALS: _____

_____

_____

_____

_____

_____

Important Dates:

Event Name_____

Date_____

Event Name_____

Date_____

Event Name_____

Date_____

Mind and Body

- Do remember to call someone you love.
- Do remember to exercise your mind and body.
- Do remember to drink plenty of water
- Do remember to get plenty of rest.

Week of _____

	Monday	Tuesday	Wednesday
5 am			
6 am			
7 am			
8 am			
9 am			
10 am			
11 am			
12 pm			
1 pm			
2 pm			
3 pm			
4 pm			
5 pm			
6 pm			
7 pm			
8 pm			
9 pm			
10 pm			
	Water ◊◊◊◊◊◊◊◊	Water ◊◊◊◊◊◊◊◊	Water ◊◊◊◊◊◊◊◊

	Thursday	Friday		Saturday
5 am			9 am	
6 am			10 am	
7 am			11 am	
8 am			12 pm	
9 am			1 pm	
10 am			2 pm	
11 am			3 pm	
12 pm			4 pm	
1 pm				Water ᎒᎒᎒᎒᎒᎒᎒
2 pm				Sunday
3 pm			9 am	
4 pm			10 am	
5 pm			11 am	
6 pm			12 pm	
7 pm			1 pm	
8 pm			2 pm	
9 pm			3 pm	
10 pm			4 pm	
	Water ᎒᎒᎒᎒᎒᎒᎒	Water ᎒᎒᎒᎒᎒᎒᎒		Water ᎒᎒᎒᎒᎒᎒᎒

Week of _____

Be joyful in hope, patient in affliction, faithful in prayer.

Romans 12:12

Prayer Request

PERSONAL REQUEST: _____
_____
_____
_____
_____

FAMILY REQUEST: _____
_____
_____
_____
_____

PROFESSIONAL REQUEST: _____
_____
_____
_____
_____
_____
_____

Goals

PERSONAL GOALS: _____

_____
_____
_____
_____
_____
_____
_____

FAMILY GOALS: _____

_____
_____
_____
_____
_____
_____

PROFESSIONAL GOALS: _____

_____
_____
_____
_____
_____
_____

Important Dates:

Event Name_____

Date_____

Event Name_____

Date_____

Event Name_____

Date_____

Mind and Body

- Do remember to call someone you love.
- Do remember to exercise your mind and body.
- Do remember to drink plenty of water
- Do remember to get plenty of rest.

Week of _____

	Monday	Tuesday	Wednesday
5 am			
6 am			
7 am			
8 am			
9 am			
10 am			
11 am			
12 pm			
1 pm			
2 pm			
3 pm			
4 pm			
5 pm			
6 pm			
7 pm			
8 pm			
9 pm			
10 pm			
	Water ◊◊◊◊◊◊◊◊	Water ◊◊◊◊◊◊◊◊	Water ◊◊◊◊◊◊◊◊

	Thursday	Friday		Saturday
5 am			9 am	
6 am			10 am	
7 am			11 am	
8 am			12 pm	
9 am			1 pm	
10 am			2 pm	
11 am			3 pm	
12 pm			4 pm	
1 pm				Water 💧💧💧💧💧💧💧💧
2 pm				Sunday
3 pm			9 am	
4 pm			10 am	
5 pm			11 am	
6 pm			12 pm	
7 pm			1 pm	
8 pm			2 pm	
9 pm			3 pm	
10 pm			4 pm	
	Water 💧💧💧💧💧💧💧💧	Water 💧💧💧💧💧💧💧💧		Water 💧💧💧💧💧💧💧

Week of _____

Shout for joy to the Lord, all the earth. Worship the Lord with gladness; come before him with joyful songs. Know that the Lord is God. It is he who made us, and we are his; we are his people, the sheep of his pasture. ...

Psalm 100

Prayer Request

PERSONAL REQUEST: _____

_____

_____

_____

_____

FAMILY REQUEST: _____

_____

_____

_____

_____

PROFESSIONAL REQUEST: _____

_____

_____

_____

_____

_____

_____

Goals

PERSONAL GOALS: _____

_____

_____

_____

_____

_____

_____

_____

FAMILY GOALS: _____

_____

_____

_____

_____

_____

PROFESSIONAL GOALS: _____

_____

_____

_____

_____

_____

Important Dates:

Event Name_____

Date_____

Event Name_____

Date_____

Event Name_____

Date_____

Mind and Body

- Do remember to call someone you love.
- Do remember to exercise your mind and body.
- Do remember to drink plenty of water
- Do remember to get plenty of rest.

Week of _____

	Monday	Tuesday	Wednesday
5 am			
6 am			
7 am			
8 am			
9 am			
10 am			
11 am			
12 pm			
1 pm			
2 pm			
3 pm			
4 pm			
5 pm			
6 pm			
7 pm			
8 pm			
9 pm			
10 pm			
	Water ○○○○○○○○	Water ○○○○○○○○	Water ○○○○○○○○

	Thursday	Friday		Saturday
5 am			9 am	
6 am			10 am	
7 am			11 am	
8 am			12 pm	
9 am			1 pm	
10 am			2 pm	
11 am			3 pm	
12 pm			4 pm	
1 pm				Water ◊◊◊◊◊◊◊◊
2 pm				Sunday
3 pm			9 am	
4 pm			10 am	
5 pm			11 am	
6 pm			12 pm	
7 pm			1 pm	
8 pm			2 pm	
9 pm			3 pm	
10 pm			4 pm	
	Water ◊◊◊◊◊◊◊◊	Water ◊◊◊◊◊◊◊◊		Water ◊◊◊◊◊◊◊◊

Week of _____

These things I have spoken to you, that my joy may be in you, and that your joy may be full.

John 15:11

Prayer Request

PERSONAL REQUEST: _____
_____
_____
_____
_____

FAMILY REQUEST: _____
_____
_____
_____
_____
_____

PROFESSIONAL REQUEST: _____
_____
_____
_____
_____
_____
_____

Goals

PERSONAL GOALS: _____

_____
_____
_____
_____
_____
_____

FAMILY GOALS: _____

_____
_____
_____
_____
_____

PROFESSIONAL GOALS: _____

_____
_____
_____
_____
_____

Important Dates:

Event Name_____
Date_____
Event Name_____
Date_____
Event Name_____
Date_____

Mind and Body

- Do remember to call someone you love.
- Do remember to exercise your mind and body.
- Do remember to drink plenty of water
- Do remember to get plenty of rest.

Week of _____

	Monday	Tuesday	Wednesday
5 am			
6 am			
7 am			
8 am			
9 am			
10 am			
11 am			
12 pm			
1 pm			
2 pm			
3 pm			
4 pm			
5 pm			
6 pm			
7 pm			
8 pm			
9 pm			
10 pm			
	Water ◊◊◊◊◊◊◊◊	Water ◊◊◊◊◊◊◊◊	Water ◊◊◊◊◊◊◊◊

	Thursday	Friday		Saturday
5 am			9 am	
6 am			10 am	
7 am			11 am	
8 am			12 pm	
9 am			1 pm	
10 am			2 pm	
11 am			3 pm	
12 pm			4 pm	
1 pm				Water ◊◊◊◊◊◊◊◊
2 pm				Sunday
3 pm			9 am	
4 pm			10 am	
5 pm			11 am	
6 pm			12 pm	
7 pm			1 pm	
8 pm			2 pm	
9 pm			3 pm	
10 pm			4 pm	
	Water ◊◊◊◊◊◊◊◊	Water ◊◊◊◊◊◊◊◊		Water ◊◊◊◊◊◊◊◊

Week of _____

When a country is rebellious, it has many rulers, but a ruler with discernment and knowledge maintains order.

Proverbs 28:2

Prayer Request

PERSONAL REQUEST: _____

_____

_____

_____

_____

FAMILY REQUEST: _____

_____

_____

_____

_____

_____

PROFESSIONAL REQUEST: _____

_____

_____

_____

_____

_____

_____

Goals

PERSONAL GOALS: _____

_____

_____

_____

_____

_____

_____

_____

FAMILY GOALS: _____

_____

_____

_____

_____

_____

PROFESSIONAL GOALS: _____

_____

_____

_____

_____

_____

Important Dates:

Event Name_____

Date_____

Event Name_____

Date_____

Event Name_____

Date_____

Mind and Body

- Do remember to call someone you love.
- Do remember to exercise your mind and body.
- Do remember to drink plenty of water
- Do remember to get plenty of rest.

Week of _____

	Monday	Tuesday	Wednesday
5 am			
6 am			
7 am			
8 am			
9 am			
10 am			
11 am			
12 pm			
1 pm			
2 pm			
3 pm			
4 pm			
5 pm			
6 pm			
7 pm			
8 pm			
9 pm			
10 pm			
	Water ◊◊◊◊◊◊◊◊	Water ◊◊◊◊◊◊◊◊	Water ◊◊◊◊◊◊◊◊

	Thursday	Friday		Saturday
5 am			9 am	
6 am			10 am	
7 am			11 am	
8 am			12 pm	
9 am			1 pm	
10 am			2 pm	
11 am			3 pm	
12 pm			4 pm	
1 pm				Water 〇〇〇〇〇〇〇〇
2 pm				Sunday
3 pm			9 am	
4 pm			10 am	
5 pm			11 am	
6 pm			12 pm	
7 pm			1 pm	
8 pm			2 pm	
9 pm			3 pm	
10 pm			4 pm	
	Water 〇〇〇〇〇〇〇〇	Water 〇〇〇〇〇〇〇〇		Water 〇〇〇〇〇〇〇〇

Week of _____

Praise be to the God and Father of our Lord Jesus Christ, who has blessed us in the heavenly realms with every spiritual blessing in Christ.

Ephesians 1:3

Prayer Request

PERSONAL REQUEST: _____

_____
_____
_____
_____

FAMILY REQUEST: _____

_____
_____
_____
_____
_____

PROFESSIONAL REQUEST: _____

_____
_____
_____
_____
_____
_____

Goals

PERSONAL GOALS: _____

_____
_____
_____
_____
_____
_____

FAMILY GOALS: _____

_____
_____
_____
_____
_____

PROFESSIONAL GOALS: _____

_____
_____
_____
_____
_____

Important Dates:

Event Name_____

Date_____

Event Name_____

Date_____

Event Name_____

Date_____

Mind and Body

- Do remember to call someone you love.
- Do remember to exercise your mind and body.
- Do remember to drink plenty of water
- Do remember to get plenty of rest.

Week of _____

	Monday	Tuesday	Wednesday
5 am			
6 am			
7 am			
8 am			
9 am			
10 am			
11 am			
12 pm			
1 pm			
2 pm			
3 pm			
4 pm			
5 pm			
6 pm			
7 pm			
8 pm			
9 pm			
10 pm			
	Water ◊◊◊◊◊◊◊◊	Water ◊◊◊◊◊◊◊◊	Water ◊◊◊◊◊◊◊◊

	Thursday	Friday		Saturday
5 am			9 am	
6 am			10 am	
7 am			11 am	
8 am			12 pm	
9 am			1 pm	
10 am			2 pm	
11 am			3 pm	
12 pm			4 pm	
1 pm				Water ◊◊◊◊◊◊◊◊
2 pm				Sunday
3 pm			9 am	
4 pm			10 am	
5 pm			11 am	
6 pm			12 pm	
7 pm			1 pm	
8 pm			2 pm	
9 pm			3 pm	
10 pm			4 pm	
	Water ◊◊◊◊◊◊◊◊	Water ◊◊◊◊◊◊◊◊		Water ◊◊◊◊◊◊◊◊

Week of _____

Therefore, as we have opportunity, let us do good to all people, especially to those who belong to the family of believers.

Galatians 6:10

Prayer Request

PERSONAL REQUEST: _____

_____

_____

_____

_____

FAMILY REQUEST: _____

_____

_____

_____

_____

_____

PROFESSIONAL REQUEST: _____

_____

_____

_____

_____

_____

_____

_____

Goals

PERSONAL GOALS: _____

_____
_____
_____
_____
_____
_____

FAMILY GOALS: _____

_____
_____
_____
_____
_____

PROFESSIONAL GOALS: _____

_____
_____
_____
_____
_____

Important Dates:

Event Name_____

Date_____

Event Name_____

Date_____

Event Name_____

Date_____

Mind and Body

- Do remember to call someone you love.
- Do remember to exercise your mind and body.
- Do remember to drink plenty of water
- Do remember to get plenty of rest.

Week of _____

	Monday	Tuesday	Wednesday
5 am			
6 am			
7 am			
8 am			
9 am			
10 am			
11 am			
12 pm			
1 pm			
2 pm			
3 pm			
4 pm			
5 pm			
6 pm			
7 pm			
8 pm			
9 pm			
10 pm			
	Water 💧💧💧💧💧💧💧💧	Water 💧💧💧💧💧💧💧💧	Water 💧💧💧💧💧💧💧💧

	Thursday	Friday		Saturday
5 am			9 am	
6 am			10 am	
7 am			11 am	
8 am			12 pm	
9 am			1 pm	
10 am			2 pm	
11 am			3 pm	
12 pm			4 pm	
1 pm				Water 󠀠◊◊◊◊◊◊◊◊
2 pm				Sunday
3 pm			9 am	
4 pm			10 am	
5 pm			11 am	
6 pm			12 pm	
7 pm			1 pm	
8 pm			2 pm	
9 pm			3 pm	
10 pm			4 pm	
	Water ◊◊◊◊◊◊◊◊	Water ◊◊◊◊◊◊◊◊		Water ◊◊◊◊◊◊◊◊

Week of _____

If you fully obey the Lord your God and carefully follow all his commands I give you today, the Lord your God will set you high above all the nations on earth.

Deuteronomy 28:1

Prayer Request

PERSONAL REQUEST: _____

_____

_____

_____

_____

FAMILY REQUEST: _____

_____

_____

_____

_____

_____

PROFESSIONAL REQUEST: _____

_____

_____

_____

_____

_____

_____

Goals

PERSONAL GOALS: _____

_____

_____

_____

_____

_____

_____

FAMILY GOALS: _____

_____

_____

_____

_____

_____

PROFESSIONAL GOALS: _____

_____

_____

_____

_____

_____

Important Dates:

Event Name_____

Date_____

Event Name_____

Date_____

Event Name_____

Date_____

Mind and Body

- Do remember to call someone you love.
- Do remember to exercise your mind and body.
- Do remember to drink plenty of water
- Do remember to get plenty of rest.

Week of _____

	Monday	Tuesday	Wednesday
5 am			
6 am			
7 am			
8 am			
9 am			
10 am			
11 am			
12 pm			
1 pm			
2 pm			
3 pm			
4 pm			
5 pm			
6 pm			
7 pm			
8 pm			
9 pm			
10 pm			
	Water ◊◊◊◊◊◊◊◊	Water ◊◊◊◊◊◊◊◊	Water ◊◊◊◊◊◊◊◊

	Thursday	Friday		Saturday
5 am			9 am	
6 am			10 am	
7 am			11 am	
8 am			12 pm	
9 am			1 pm	
10 am			2 pm	
11 am			3 pm	
12 pm			4 pm	
1 pm				Water 💧💧💧💧💧💧💧
2 pm				Sunday
3 pm			9 am	
4 pm			10 am	
5 pm			11 am	
6 pm			12 pm	
7 pm			1 pm	
8 pm			2 pm	
9 pm			3 pm	
10 pm			4 pm	
	Water 💧💧💧💧💧💧💧	Water 💧💧💧💧💧💧💧		Water 💧💧💧💧💧💧💧

Week of _____

You will eat the fruit of your labor; blessings and prosperity will be yours.

Psalm 128:2

Prayer Request

PERSONAL REQUEST: _____

_____

_____

_____

_____

FAMILY REQUEST: _____

_____

_____

_____

_____

_____

PROFESSIONAL REQUEST: _____

_____

_____

_____

_____

_____

_____

Goals

PERSONAL GOALS: _____

_____

_____

_____

_____

_____

_____

FAMILY GOALS: _____

_____

_____

_____

_____

_____

PROFESSIONAL GOALS: _____

_____

_____

_____

_____

_____

_____

Important Dates:

Event Name_____

Date_____

Event Name_____

Date_____

Event Name_____

Date_____

Mind and Body

- Do remember to call someone you love.
- Do remember to exercise your mind and body.
- Do remember to drink plenty of water
- Do remember to get plenty of rest.

Week of _____

	Monday	Tuesday	Wednesday
5 am			
6 am			
7 am			
8 am			
9 am			
10 am			
11 am			
12 pm			
1 pm			
2 pm			
3 pm			
4 pm			
5 pm			
6 pm			
7 pm			
8 pm			
9 pm			
10 pm			
	Water 💧💧💧💧💧💧💧💧	Water 💧💧💧💧💧💧💧💧	Water 💧💧💧💧💧💧💧💧

	Thursday	Friday		Saturday
5 am			9 am	
6 am			10 am	
7 am			11 am	
8 am			12 pm	
9 am			1 pm	
10 am			2 pm	
11 am			3 pm	
12 pm			4 pm	
1 pm				Water 󠀠◊◊◊◊◊◊◊◊
2 pm				Sunday
3 pm			9 am	
4 pm			10 am	
5 pm			11 am	
6 pm			12 pm	
7 pm			1 pm	
8 pm			2 pm	
9 pm			3 pm	
10 pm			4 pm	
	Water ◊◊◊◊◊◊◊◊	Water ◊◊◊◊◊◊◊◊		Water ◊◊◊◊◊◊◊◊

Week of _____

I always thank my God for you because of his grace given you in Christ Jesus.

1 Corinthians 1:4

Prayer Request

PERSONAL REQUEST: _____
_____
_____
_____
_____

FAMILY REQUEST: _____
_____
_____
_____
_____
_____
_____

PROFESSIONAL REQUEST: _____
_____
_____
_____
_____
_____
_____

Goals

PERSONAL GOALS: _____

_____

_____

_____

_____

_____

_____

FAMILY GOALS: _____

_____

_____

_____

_____

_____

PROFESSIONAL GOALS: _____

_____

_____

_____

_____

_____

_____

Important Dates:

Event Name_____

Date_____

Event Name_____

Date_____

Event Name_____

Date_____

Mind and Body

- Do remember to call someone you love.
- Do remember to exercise your mind and body.
- Do remember to drink plenty of water
- Do remember to get plenty of rest.

Week of _____

	Monday	Tuesday	Wednesday
5 am			
6 am			
7 am			
8 am			
9 am			
10 am			
11 am			
12 pm			
1 pm			
2 pm			
3 pm			
4 pm			
5 pm			
6 pm			
7 pm			
8 pm			
9 pm			
10 pm			
	Water ◊◊◊◊◊◊◊◊	Water ◊◊◊◊◊◊◊◊	Water ◊◊◊◊◊◊◊◊

	Thursday	Friday		Saturday
5 am			9 am	
6 am			10 am	
7 am			11 am	
8 am			12 pm	
9 am			1 pm	
10 am			2 pm	
11 am			3 pm	
12 pm			4 pm	
1 pm				Water 󠀠󠀠󠀠󠀠󠀠󠀠󠀠󠀠
2 pm				Sunday
3 pm			9 am	
4 pm			10 am	
5 pm			11 am	
6 pm			12 pm	
7 pm			1 pm	
8 pm			2 pm	
9 pm			3 pm	
10 pm			4 pm	
	Water	Water		Water

Week of _____

We ought always to thank God for you, brothers and sisters, and rightly so, because your faith is growing more and more, and the love all of you have for one another is increasing.

2 Thessalonians 1:3

Prayer Request

PERSONAL REQUEST: _____

_____

_____

_____

_____

FAMILY REQUEST: _____

_____

_____

_____

_____

_____

PROFESSIONAL REQUEST: _____

_____

_____

_____

_____

_____

Goals

PERSONAL GOALS: _____

_____

_____

_____

_____

_____

_____

FAMILY GOALS: _____

_____

_____

_____

_____

_____

PROFESSIONAL GOALS: _____

_____

_____

_____

_____

_____

Important Dates:

Event Name_____

Date_____

Event Name_____

Date_____

Event Name_____

Date_____

Mind and Body

- Do remember to call someone you love.
- Do remember to exercise your mind and body.
- Do remember to drink plenty of water
- Do remember to get plenty of rest.

Week of _____

	Monday	Tuesday	Wednesday
5 am			
6 am			
7 am			
8 am			
9 am			
10 am			
11 am			
12 pm			
1 pm			
2 pm			
3 pm			
4 pm			
5 pm			
6 pm			
7 pm			
8 pm			
9 pm			
10 pm			
	Water ⬦⬦⬦⬦⬦⬦⬦⬦	Water ⬦⬦⬦⬦⬦⬦⬦⬦	Water ⬦⬦⬦⬦⬦⬦⬦⬦

	Thursday	Friday		Saturday
5 am			9 am	
6 am			10 am	
7 am			11 am	
8 am			12 pm	
9 am			1 pm	
10 am			2 pm	
11 am			3 pm	
12 pm			4 pm	
1 pm				Water 💧💧💧💧💧💧💧💧
2 pm				Sunday
3 pm			9 am	
4 pm			10 am	
5 pm			11 am	
6 pm			12 pm	
7 pm			1 pm	
8 pm			2 pm	
9 pm			3 pm	
10 pm			4 pm	
	Water 💧💧💧💧💧💧💧💧	Water 💧💧💧💧💧💧💧💧		Water 💧💧💧💧💧💧💧💧

Week of _____

Be devoted to one another in love. Honor one another above yourselves.

Romans 12:10

Prayer Request

PERSONAL REQUEST: _____

FAMILY REQUEST: _____

PROFESSIONAL REQUEST: _____

Goals

PERSONAL GOALS: _____

_____

_____

_____

_____

_____

_____

FAMILY GOALS: _____

_____

_____

_____

_____

_____

PROFESSIONAL GOALS: _____

_____

_____

_____

_____

_____

Important Dates:

Event Name_____

Date_____

Event Name_____

Date_____

Event Name_____

Date_____

Mind and Body

- Do remember to call someone you love.
- Do remember to exercise your mind and body.
- Do remember to drink plenty of water
- Do remember to get plenty of rest.

Week of _____

	Monday	Tuesday	Wednesday
5 am			
6 am			
7 am			
8 am			
9 am			
10 am			
11 am			
12 pm			
1 pm			
2 pm			
3 pm			
4 pm			
5 pm			
6 pm			
7 pm			
8 pm			
9 pm			
10 pm			
	Water 💧💧💧💧💧💧💧💧	Water 💧💧💧💧💧💧💧💧	Water 💧💧💧💧💧💧💧💧

	Thursday	Friday		Saturday
5 am			9 am	
6 am			10 am	
7 am			11 am	
8 am			12 pm	
9 am			1 pm	
10 am			2 pm	
11 am			3 pm	
12 pm			4 pm	
1 pm				Water 󰀀󰀀󰀀󰀀󰀀󰀀󰀀󰀀
2 pm				Sunday
3 pm			9 am	
4 pm			10 am	
5 pm			11 am	
6 pm			12 pm	
7 pm			1 pm	
8 pm			2 pm	
9 pm			3 pm	
10 pm			4 pm	
	Water 󰀀󰀀󰀀󰀀󰀀󰀀󰀀󰀀	Water 󰀀󰀀󰀀󰀀󰀀󰀀󰀀󰀀		Water 󰀀󰀀󰀀󰀀󰀀󰀀󰀀󰀀

Week of _____

"Do not let your heart be troubled; believe in God, believe also in Me.
John 14:1

Prayer Request

PERSONAL REQUEST: _____

_____

_____

_____

_____

FAMILY REQUEST: _____

_____

_____

_____

_____

_____

PROFESSIONAL REQUEST: _____

_____

_____

_____

_____

_____

_____

_____

Goals

PERSONAL GOALS: _____

_____

_____

_____

_____

_____

_____

FAMILY GOALS: _____

_____

_____

_____

_____

_____

PROFESSIONAL GOALS: _____

_____

_____

_____

_____

_____

Important Dates:

Event Name_____

Date_____

Event Name_____

Date_____

Event Name_____

Date_____

Mind and Body

- Do remember to call someone you love.
- Do remember to exercise your mind and body.
- Do remember to drink plenty of water
- Do remember to get plenty of rest.

Week of _____

	Monday	Tuesday	Wednesday
5 am			
6 am			
7 am			
8 am			
9 am			
10 am			
11 am			
12 pm			
1 pm			
2 pm			
3 pm			
4 pm			
5 pm			
6 pm			
7 pm			
8 pm			
9 pm			
10 pm			
	Water 💧💧💧💧💧💧💧💧	Water 💧💧💧💧💧💧💧💧	Water 💧💧💧💧💧💧💧💧

	Thursday	Friday		Saturday
5 am			9 am	
6 am			10 am	
7 am			11 am	
8 am			12 pm	
9 am			1 pm	
10 am			2 pm	
11 am			3 pm	
12 pm			4 pm	
1 pm				Water 🜄🜄🜄🜄🜄🜄🜄
2 pm				Sunday
3 pm			9 am	
4 pm			10 am	
5 pm			11 am	
6 pm			12 pm	
7 pm			1 pm	
8 pm			2 pm	
9 pm			3 pm	
10 pm			4 pm	
	Water 🜄🜄🜄🜄🜄🜄🜄	Water 🜄🜄🜄🜄🜄🜄🜄		Water 🜄🜄🜄🜄🜄🜄🜄

Week of _____

"Trust in the LORD forever, For in GOD the LORD, we have an everlasting Rock.

Isaiah 26:4

Prayer Request

PERSONAL REQUEST: _____

_____

_____

_____

_____

FAMILY REQUEST: _____

_____

_____

_____

_____

_____

PROFESSIONAL REQUEST: _____

_____

_____

_____

_____

_____

_____

Goals

PERSONAL GOALS: _____

_____

_____

_____

_____

_____

_____

FAMILY GOALS: _____

_____

_____

_____

_____

_____

PROFESSIONAL GOALS: _____

_____

_____

_____

_____

_____

Important Dates:

Event Name_____

Date_____

Event Name_____

Date_____

Event Name_____

Date_____

Mind and Body

- Do remember to call someone you love.
- Do remember to exercise your mind and body.
- Do remember to drink plenty of water
- Do remember to get plenty of rest.

Week of _____

	Monday	Tuesday	Wednesday
5 am			
6 am			
7 am			
8 am			
9 am			
10 am			
11 am			
12 pm			
1 pm			
2 pm			
3 pm			
4 pm			
5 pm			
6 pm			
7 pm			
8 pm			
9 pm			
10 pm			
	Water ⬦⬦⬦⬦⬦⬦⬦⬦	Water ⬦⬦⬦⬦⬦⬦⬦⬦	Water ⬦⬦⬦⬦⬦⬦⬦⬦

	Thursday	Friday		Saturday
5 am			9 am	
6 am			10 am	
7 am			11 am	
8 am			12 pm	
9 am			1 pm	
10 am			2 pm	
11 am			3 pm	
12 pm			4 pm	
1 pm			Water	○○○○○○○○
2 pm			Sunday	
3 pm			9 am	
4 pm			10 am	
5 pm			11 am	
6 pm			12 pm	
7 pm			1 pm	
8 pm			2 pm	
9 pm			3 pm	
10 pm			4 pm	
	Water ○○○○○○○○	Water ○○○○○○○○		Water ○○○○○○○○

Week of _____

Then my soul will rejoice in the Lord and delight in his salvation.

Psalm 35:9

Prayer Request

PERSONAL REQUEST: _____
_____
_____
_____
_____

FAMILY REQUEST: _____
_____
_____
_____
_____
_____

PROFESSIONAL REQUEST: _____
_____
_____
_____
_____
_____
_____

Goals

PERSONAL GOALS: _____

_____
_____
_____
_____
_____
_____
_____

FAMILY GOALS: _____

_____
_____
_____
_____
_____
_____

PROFESSIONAL GOALS: _____

_____
_____
_____
_____
_____
_____

Important Dates:

Event Name_____

Date_____

Event Name_____

Date_____

Event Name_____

Date_____

Mind and Body

- Do remember to call someone you love.
- Do remember to exercise your mind and body.
- Do remember to drink plenty of water
- Do remember to get plenty of rest.

Week of _____

	Monday	Tuesday	Wednesday
5 am			
6 am			
7 am			
8 am			
9 am			
10 am			
11 am			
12 pm			
1 pm			
2 pm			
3 pm			
4 pm			
5 pm			
6 pm			
7 pm			
8 pm			
9 pm			
10 pm			
	Water ۵۵۵۵۵۵۵۵	Water ۵۵۵۵۵۵۵۵	Water ۵۵۵۵۵۵۵۵

	Thursday	Friday		Saturday
5 am			9 am	
6 am			10 am	
7 am			11 am	
8 am			12 pm	
9 am			1 pm	
10 am			2 pm	
11 am			3 pm	
12 pm			4 pm	
1 pm				Water ◊◊◊◊◊◊◊◊
2 pm				Sunday
3 pm			9 am	
4 pm			10 am	
5 pm			11 am	
6 pm			12 pm	
7 pm			1 pm	
8 pm			2 pm	
9 pm			3 pm	
10 pm			4 pm	
	Water ◊◊◊◊◊◊◊◊	Water ◊◊◊◊◊◊◊◊		Water ◊◊◊◊◊◊◊

Week of _____

Walk in obedience to all that the Lord your God has commanded you, so that you may live and prosper and prolong your days in the land that you will possess.

Deuteronomy 5:33

Prayer Request

PERSONAL REQUEST: _____

_____

_____

_____

_____

FAMILY REQUEST: _____

_____

_____

_____

_____

_____

PROFESSIONAL REQUEST: _____

_____

_____

_____

_____

_____

_____

Goals

PERSONAL GOALS: _____

_____

_____

_____

_____

_____

_____

_____

FAMILY GOALS: _____

_____

_____

_____

_____

_____

_____

PROFESSIONAL GOALS: _____

_____

_____

_____

_____

_____

_____

Important Dates:

Event Name_____

Date_____

Event Name_____

Date_____

Event Name_____

Date_____

Mind and Body

- Do remember to call someone you love.
- Do remember to exercise your mind and body.
- Do remember to drink plenty of water
- Do remember to get plenty of rest.

Week of _____

	Monday	Tuesday	Wednesday
5 am			
6 am			
7 am			
8 am			
9 am			
10 am			
11 am			
12 pm			
1 pm			
2 pm			
3 pm			
4 pm			
5 pm			
6 pm			
7 pm			
8 pm			
9 pm			
10 pm			
	Water ◊◊◊◊◊◊◊◊	Water ◊◊◊◊◊◊◊◊	Water ◊◊◊◊◊◊◊◊

	Thursday	Friday		Saturday
5 am			9 am	
6 am			10 am	
7 am			11 am	
8 am			12 pm	
9 am			1 pm	
10 am			2 pm	
11 am			3 pm	
12 pm			4 pm	
1 pm				Water 💧💧💧💧💧💧💧
2 pm				Sunday
3 pm			9 am	
4 pm			10 am	
5 pm			11 am	
6 pm			12 pm	
7 pm			1 pm	
8 pm			2 pm	
9 pm			3 pm	
10 pm			4 pm	
	Water 💧💧💧💧💧💧💧	Water 💧💧💧💧💧💧💧		Water 💧💧💧💧💧💧

Week of _____

I wait for the Lord, my soul waits, and in his word I put my hope.
Psalm 130:5

Prayer Request

PERSONAL REQUEST: _____

FAMILY REQUEST: _____

PROFESSIONAL REQUEST: _____

Goals

PERSONAL GOALS: _____

_____

_____

_____

_____

_____

_____

FAMILY GOALS: _____

_____

_____

_____

_____

_____

PROFESSIONAL GOALS: _____

_____

_____

_____

_____

_____

Important Dates:

Event Name_____

Date_____

Event Name_____

Date_____

Event Name_____

Date_____

Mind and Body

- Do remember to call someone you love.
- Do remember to exercise your mind and body.
- Do remember to drink plenty of water
- Do remember to get plenty of rest.

Week of _____

	Monday	Tuesday	Wednesday
5 am			
6 am			
7 am			
8 am			
9 am			
10 am			
11 am			
12 pm			
1 pm			
2 pm			
3 pm			
4 pm			
5 pm			
6 pm			
7 pm			
8 pm			
9 pm			
10 pm			
	Water ᶿ ᶿ ᶿ ᶿ ᶿ ᶿ ᶿ ᶿ	Water ᶿ ᶿ ᶿ ᶿ ᶿ ᶿ ᶿ ᶿ	Water ᶿ ᶿ ᶿ ᶿ ᶿ ᶿ ᶿ ᶿ

	Thursday	Friday		Saturday
5 am			9 am	
6 am			10 am	
7 am			11 am	
8 am			12 pm	
9 am			1 pm	
10 am			2 pm	
11 am			3 pm	
12 pm			4 pm	
1 pm				Water ◊◊◊◊◊◊◊◊
2 pm				Sunday
3 pm			9 am	
4 pm			10 am	
5 pm			11 am	
6 pm			12 pm	
7 pm			1 pm	
8 pm			2 pm	
9 pm			3 pm	
10 pm			4 pm	
	Water ◊◊◊◊◊◊◊◊	Water ◊◊◊◊◊◊◊◊		Water ◊◊◊◊◊◊◊◊

Week of _____

All Scripture is God-breathed and is useful for teaching, rebuking, correcting and training in righteousness,

> 2 Timothy 3:16

Prayer Request

PERSONAL REQUEST: _____

_____

_____

_____

_____

FAMILY REQUEST: _____

_____

_____

_____

_____

PROFESSIONAL REQUEST: _____

_____

_____

_____

_____

_____

_____

Goals

PERSONAL GOALS: _____

_____

_____

_____

_____

_____

_____

FAMILY GOALS: _____

_____

_____

_____

_____

_____

PROFESSIONAL GOALS: _____

_____

_____

_____

_____

_____

_____

Important Dates:

Event Name_____

Date_____

Event Name_____

Date_____

Event Name_____

Date_____

Mind and Body

- Do remember to call someone you love.
- Do remember to exercise your mind and body.
- Do remember to drink plenty of water
- Do remember to get plenty of rest.

Week of _____

	Monday	Tuesday	Wednesday
5 am			
6 am			
7 am			
8 am			
9 am			
10 am			
11 am			
12 pm			
1 pm			
2 pm			
3 pm			
4 pm			
5 pm			
6 pm			
7 pm			
8 pm			
9 pm			
10 pm			
	Water ߜߜߜߜߜߜߜߜ	Water ߜߜߜߜߜߜߜߜ	Water ߜߜߜߜߜߜߜߜ

	Thursday	Friday		Saturday
5 am			9 am	
6 am			10 am	
7 am			11 am	
8 am			12 pm	
9 am			1 pm	
10 am			2 pm	
11 am			3 pm	
12 pm			4 pm	
1 pm				Water 💧💧💧💧💧💧💧
2 pm				Sunday
3 pm			9 am	
4 pm			10 am	
5 pm			11 am	
6 pm			12 pm	
7 pm			1 pm	
8 pm			2 pm	
9 pm			3 pm	
10 pm			4 pm	
	Water 💧💧💧💧💧💧💧	Water 💧💧💧💧💧💧💧		Water 💧💧💧💧💧💧💧

Week of _____

For this reason, since the day we heard about you, we have not stopped praying for you. We continually ask God to fill you with the knowledge of his will through all the wisdom and understanding that the Spirit gives,

Colossians 1:9

Prayer Request

PERSONAL REQUEST: _____

_____

_____

_____

_____

FAMILY REQUEST: _____

_____

_____

_____

_____

_____

PROFESSIONAL REQUEST: _____

_____

_____

_____

_____

_____

_____

Goals

PERSONAL GOALS: _____

_____

_____

_____

_____

_____

_____

FAMILY GOALS: _____

_____

_____

_____

_____

_____

PROFESSIONAL GOALS: _____

_____

_____

_____

_____

_____

Important Dates:

Event Name_____

Date_____

Event Name_____

Date_____

Event Name_____

Date_____

Mind and Body

- Do remember to call someone you love.
- Do remember to exercise your mind and body.
- Do remember to drink plenty of water
- Do remember to get plenty of rest.

Week of _____

	Monday	Tuesday	Wednesday
5 am			
6 am			
7 am			
8 am			
9 am			
10 am			
11 am			
12 pm			
1 pm			
2 pm			
3 pm			
4 pm			
5 pm			
6 pm			
7 pm			
8 pm			
9 pm			
10 pm			
	Water ٨٨٨٨٨٨٨٨	Water ٨٨٨٨٨٨٨٨	Water ٨٨٨٨٨٨٨٨

	Thursday	Friday		Saturday
5 am			9 am	
6 am			10 am	
7 am			11 am	
8 am			12 pm	
9 am			1 pm	
10 am			2 pm	
11 am			3 pm	
12 pm			4 pm	
1 pm				Water 💧💧💧💧💧💧💧
2 pm				Sunday
3 pm			9 am	
4 pm			10 am	
5 pm			11 am	
6 pm			12 pm	
7 pm			1 pm	
8 pm			2 pm	
9 pm			3 pm	
10 pm			4 pm	
	Water 💧💧💧💧💧💧💧	Water 💧💧💧💧💧💧💧		Water 💧💧💧💧💧💧

Week of _____

Cast your cares on the Lord and he will sustain you; he will never let the righteous fall.

Psalm 55:22

Prayer Request

PERSONAL REQUEST: _____

_____

_____

_____

_____

FAMILY REQUEST: _____

_____

_____

_____

_____

_____

PROFESSIONAL REQUEST: _____

_____

_____

_____

_____

_____

_____

Goals

PERSONAL GOALS: _____

_____

_____

_____

_____

_____

_____

FAMILY GOALS: _____

_____

_____

_____

_____

_____

PROFESSIONAL GOALS: _____

_____

_____

_____

_____

_____

Important Dates:

Event Name_____

Date_____

Event Name_____

Date_____

Event Name_____

Date_____

Mind and Body

- Do remember to call someone you love.
- Do remember to exercise your mind and body.
- Do remember to drink plenty of water
- Do remember to get plenty of rest.

Week of _____

	Monday	Tuesday	Wednesday
5 am			
6 am			
7 am			
8 am			
9 am			
10 am			
11 am			
12 pm			
1 pm			
2 pm			
3 pm			
4 pm			
5 pm			
6 pm			
7 pm			
8 pm			
9 pm			
10 pm			
	Water ͏ ͏ ͏ ͏ ͏ ͏ ͏ ͏	Water ͏ ͏ ͏ ͏ ͏ ͏ ͏ ͏	Water ͏ ͏ ͏ ͏ ͏ ͏ ͏ ͏

	Thursday	Friday		Saturday
5 am			9 am	
6 am			10 am	
7 am			11 am	
8 am			12 pm	
9 am			1 pm	
10 am			2 pm	
11 am			3 pm	
12 pm			4 pm	
1 pm				Water 💧💧💧💧💧💧💧
2 pm				Sunday
3 pm			9 am	
4 pm			10 am	
5 pm			11 am	
6 pm			12 pm	
7 pm			1 pm	
8 pm			2 pm	
9 pm			3 pm	
10 pm			4 pm	
	Water 💧💧💧💧💧💧💧💧	Water 💧💧💧💧💧💧💧💧		Water 💧💧💧💧💧💧💧

Week of _____

"In your anger do not sin": Do not let the sun go down while you are still angry,

Ephesians 4:26

Prayer Request

PERSONAL REQUEST: _____

_____

_____

_____

_____

FAMILY REQUEST: _____

_____

_____

_____

_____

_____

PROFESSIONAL REQUEST: _____

_____

_____

_____

_____

_____

_____

Goals

PERSONAL GOALS: _____

_____

_____

_____

_____

_____

_____

FAMILY GOALS: _____

_____

_____

_____

_____

_____

PROFESSIONAL GOALS: _____

_____

_____

_____

_____

_____

Important Dates:

Event Name_____

Date_____

Event Name_____

Date_____

Event Name_____

Date_____

Mind and Body

- Do remember to call someone you love.
- Do remember to exercise your mind and body.
- Do remember to drink plenty of water
- Do remember to get plenty of rest.

Week of _____

	Monday	Tuesday	Wednesday
5 am			
6 am			
7 am			
8 am			
9 am			
10 am			
11 am			
12 pm			
1 pm			
2 pm			
3 pm			
4 pm			
5 pm			
6 pm			
7 pm			
8 pm			
9 pm			
10 pm			
	Water 💧💧💧💧💧💧💧💧	Water 💧💧💧💧💧💧💧💧	Water 💧💧💧💧💧💧💧💧

	Thursday	Friday		Saturday
5 am			9 am	
6 am			10 am	
7 am			11 am	
8 am			12 pm	
9 am			1 pm	
10 am			2 pm	
11 am			3 pm	
12 pm			4 pm	
1 pm				Water 💧💧💧💧💧💧💧
2 pm				Sunday
3 pm			9 am	
4 pm			10 am	
5 pm			11 am	
6 pm			12 pm	
7 pm			1 pm	
8 pm			2 pm	
9 pm			3 pm	
10 pm			4 pm	
	Water 💧💧💧💧💧💧💧💧	Water 💧💧💧💧💧💧💧💧		Water 💧💧💧💧💧💧💧

Week of _____

He who refreshes others will himself be refreshed.

Proverbs 11:25

Prayer Request

PERSONAL REQUEST: _____

_____

_____

_____

_____

FAMILY REQUEST: _____

_____

_____

_____

_____

_____

PROFESSIONAL REQUEST: _____

_____

_____

_____

_____

_____

_____

Goals

PERSONAL GOALS: _____

_____

_____

_____

_____

_____

_____

FAMILY GOALS: _____

_____

_____

_____

_____

_____

PROFESSIONAL GOALS: _____

_____

_____

_____

_____

_____

Important Dates:

Event Name_____

Date_____

Event Name_____

Date_____

Event Name_____

Date_____

Mind and Body

- Do remember to call someone you love.
- Do remember to exercise your mind and body.
- Do remember to drink plenty of water
- Do remember to get plenty of rest.

Week of _____

	Monday	Tuesday	Wednesday
5 am			
6 am			
7 am			
8 am			
9 am			
10 am			
11 am			
12 pm			
1 pm			
2 pm			
3 pm			
4 pm			
5 pm			
6 pm			
7 pm			
8 pm			
9 pm			
10 pm			
	Water ◊◊◊◊◊◊◊◊	Water ◊◊◊◊◊◊◊◊	Water ◊◊◊◊◊◊◊◊

	Thursday	Friday		Saturday
5 am			9 am	
6 am			10 am	
7 am			11 am	
8 am			12 pm	
9 am			1 pm	
10 am			2 pm	
11 am			3 pm	
12 pm			4 pm	
1 pm				Water 󠀠💧💧💧💧💧💧💧
2 pm				Sunday
3 pm			9 am	
4 pm			10 am	
5 pm			11 am	
6 pm			12 pm	
7 pm			1 pm	
8 pm			2 pm	
9 pm			3 pm	
10 pm			4 pm	
	Water 💧💧💧💧💧💧💧	Water 💧💧💧💧💧💧💧		Water 💧💧💧💧💧💧💧

Week of _____

Finally, be strong in the Lord and in his mighty power. Put on the full armor of God, so that you can take your stand against the devil's schemes.

Ephesians 6:10-11

Prayer Request

PERSONAL REQUEST: _____
_____
_____
_____
_____

FAMILY REQUEST: _____
_____
_____
_____
_____
_____

PROFESSIONAL REQUEST: _____
_____
_____
_____
_____
_____
_____

Goals

PERSONAL GOALS: _____

_____

_____

_____

_____

_____

_____

FAMILY GOALS: _____

_____

_____

_____

_____

_____

PROFESSIONAL GOALS: _____

_____

_____

_____

_____

_____

_____

Important Dates:

Event Name_____

Date_____

Event Name_____

Date_____

Event Name_____

Date_____

Mind and Body

- Do remember to call someone you love.
- Do remember to exercise your mind and body.
- Do remember to drink plenty of water
- Do remember to get plenty of rest.

Week of _____

	Monday	Tuesday	Wednesday
5 am			
6 am			
7 am			
8 am			
9 am			
10 am			
11 am			
12 pm			
1 pm			
2 pm			
3 pm			
4 pm			
5 pm			
6 pm			
7 pm			
8 pm			
9 pm			
10 pm			
	Water ◊◊◊◊◊◊◊◊	Water ◊◊◊◊◊◊◊◊	Water ◊◊◊◊◊◊◊◊

	Thursday	Friday		Saturday
5 am			9 am	
6 am			10 am	
7 am			11 am	
8 am			12 pm	
9 am			1 pm	
10 am			2 pm	
11 am			3 pm	
12 pm			4 pm	
1 pm				Water △△△△△△△
2 pm				Sunday
3 pm			9 am	
4 pm			10 am	
5 pm			11 am	
6 pm			12 pm	
7 pm			1 pm	
8 pm			2 pm	
9 pm			3 pm	
10 pm			4 pm	
	Water △△△△△△△	Water △△△△△△△		Water △△△△△△△

Week of _____

Blessed are those who find wisdom, those who gain understanding, for she is more profitable than silver and yields better returns than gold.

Proverbs 3:13-14

Prayer Request

PERSONAL REQUEST: _____

_____

_____

_____

_____

FAMILY REQUEST: _____

_____

_____

_____

_____

_____

PROFESSIONAL REQUEST: _____

_____

_____

_____

_____

_____

_____

Goals

PERSONAL GOALS: _____

_____

_____

_____

_____

_____

_____

FAMILY GOALS: _____

_____

_____

_____

_____

_____

PROFESSIONAL GOALS: _____

_____

_____

_____

_____

_____

_____

Important Dates:

Event Name_____

Date_____

Event Name_____

Date_____

Event Name_____

Date_____

Mind and Body

- Do remember to call someone you love.
- Do remember to exercise your mind and body.
- Do remember to drink plenty of water
- Do remember to get plenty of rest.

Week of _____

	Monday	Tuesday	Wednesday
5 am			
6 am			
7 am			
8 am			
9 am			
10 am			
11 am			
12 pm			
1 pm			
2 pm			
3 pm			
4 pm			
5 pm			
6 pm			
7 pm			
8 pm			
9 pm			
10 pm			
	Water ◊◊◊◊◊◊◊◊	Water ◊◊◊◊◊◊◊◊	Water ◊◊◊◊◊◊◊◊

	Thursday	Friday		Saturday
5 am			9 am	
6 am			10 am	
7 am			11 am	
8 am			12 pm	
9 am			1 pm	
10 am			2 pm	
11 am			3 pm	
12 pm			4 pm	
1 pm				Water 〇〇〇〇〇〇〇〇
2 pm				Sunday
3 pm			9 am	
4 pm			10 am	
5 pm			11 am	
6 pm			12 pm	
7 pm			1 pm	
8 pm			2 pm	
9 pm			3 pm	
10 pm			4 pm	
	Water 〇〇〇〇〇〇〇〇	Water 〇〇〇〇〇〇〇〇		Water 〇〇〇〇〇〇〇〇

Week of _____

But grow in the grace and knowledge of our Lord and Savior Jesus Christ. To him be glory both now and forever! Amen.

2 Peter 3:18

Prayer Request

PERSONAL REQUEST: _____

_____
_____
_____
_____

FAMILY REQUEST: _____

_____
_____
_____
_____
_____

PROFESSIONAL REQUEST: _____

_____
_____
_____
_____
_____
_____

Goals

PERSONAL GOALS: _____

_____

_____

_____

_____

_____

_____

FAMILY GOALS: _____

_____

_____

_____

_____

_____

PROFESSIONAL GOALS: _____

_____

_____

_____

_____

_____

Important Dates:

Event Name_____

Date_____

Event Name_____

Date_____

Event Name_____

Date_____

Mind and Body

- Do remember to call someone you love.
- Do remember to exercise your mind and body.
- Do remember to drink plenty of water
- Do remember to get plenty of rest.

Week of _____

	Monday	Tuesday	Wednesday
5 am			
6 am			
7 am			
8 am			
9 am			
10 am			
11 am			
12 pm			
1 pm			
2 pm			
3 pm			
4 pm			
5 pm			
6 pm			
7 pm			
8 pm			
9 pm			
10 pm			
	Water ◊◊◊◊◊◊◊◊	Water ◊◊◊◊◊◊◊◊	Water ◊◊◊◊◊◊◊◊

	Thursday	Friday		Saturday
5 am			9 am	
6 am			10 am	
7 am			11 am	
8 am			12 pm	
9 am			1 pm	
10 am			2 pm	
11 am			3 pm	
12 pm			4 pm	
1 pm				Water 💧💧💧💧💧💧💧💧
2 pm				Sunday
3 pm			9 am	
4 pm			10 am	
5 pm			11 am	
6 pm			12 pm	
7 pm			1 pm	
8 pm			2 pm	
9 pm			3 pm	
10 pm			4 pm	
	Water 💧💧💧💧💧💧💧💧	Water 💧💧💧💧💧💧💧💧		Water 💧💧💧💧💧💧💧💧

Week of _____

In the same way, faith by itself, if it is not accompanied by action, is dead.

James 2:17

Prayer Request

PERSONAL REQUEST: _____

_____

_____

_____

_____

FAMILY REQUEST: _____

_____

_____

_____

_____

_____

PROFESSIONAL REQUEST: _____

_____

_____

_____

_____

_____

_____

Goals

PERSONAL GOALS: _____

_____

_____

_____

_____

_____

_____

FAMILY GOALS: _____

_____

_____

_____

_____

_____

PROFESSIONAL GOALS: _____

_____

_____

_____

_____

_____

Important Dates:

Event Name_____

Date_____

Event Name_____

Date_____

Event Name_____

Date_____

Mind and Body

- Do remember to call someone you love.
- Do remember to exercise your mind and body.
- Do remember to drink plenty of water
- Do remember to get plenty of rest.

Week of _____

	Monday	Tuesday	Wednesday
5 am			
6 am			
7 am			
8 am			
9 am			
10 am			
11 am			
12 pm			
1 pm			
2 pm			
3 pm			
4 pm			
5 pm			
6 pm			
7 pm			
8 pm			
9 pm			
10 pm			
	Water ᶿᶿᶿᶿᶿᶿᶿᶿ	Water ᶿᶿᶿᶿᶿᶿᶿᶿ	Water ᶿᶿᶿᶿᶿᶿᶿᶿ

	Thursday	Friday		Saturday
5 am			9 am	
6 am			10 am	
7 am			11 am	
8 am			12 pm	
9 am			1 pm	
10 am			2 pm	
11 am			3 pm	
12 pm			4 pm	
1 pm				Water ooooooo
2 pm				Sunday
3 pm			9 am	
4 pm			10 am	
5 pm			11 am	
6 pm			12 pm	
7 pm			1 pm	
8 pm			2 pm	
9 pm			3 pm	
10 pm			4 pm	
	Water ooooooo	Water ooooooo		Water ooooooo

Week of _____

Live in harmony with one another. Do not be proud, but be willing to associate with people of low position. Do not be conceited.

Romans 12:16

Prayer Request

PERSONAL REQUEST: _____

_____

_____

_____

_____

FAMILY REQUEST: _____

_____

_____

_____

_____

_____

PROFESSIONAL REQUEST: _____

_____

_____

_____

_____

_____

_____

Goals

PERSONAL GOALS: _____

_____

_____

_____

_____

_____

_____

FAMILY GOALS: _____

_____

_____

_____

_____

_____

PROFESSIONAL GOALS: _____

_____

_____

_____

_____

_____

Important Dates:

Event Name_____

Date_____

Event Name_____

Date_____

Event Name_____

Date_____

Mind and Body

- Do remember to call someone you love.
- Do remember to exercise your mind and body.
- Do remember to drink plenty of water
- Do remember to get plenty of rest.

Week of _____

	Monday	Tuesday	Wednesday
5 am			
6 am			
7 am			
8 am			
9 am			
10 am			
11 am			
12 pm			
1 pm			
2 pm			
3 pm			
4 pm			
5 pm			
6 pm			
7 pm			
8 pm			
9 pm			
10 pm			
	Water ◊◊◊◊◊◊◊◊	Water ◊◊◊◊◊◊◊◊	Water ◊◊◊◊◊◊◊◊

	Thursday	Friday		Saturday
5 am			9 am	
6 am			10 am	
7 am			11 am	
8 am			12 pm	
9 am			1 pm	
10 am			2 pm	
11 am			3 pm	
12 pm			4 pm	
1 pm				Water 💧💧💧💧💧💧💧💧
2 pm				Sunday
3 pm			9 am	
4 pm			10 am	
5 pm			11 am	
6 pm			12 pm	
7 pm			1 pm	
8 pm			2 pm	
9 pm			3 pm	
10 pm			4 pm	
	Water 💧💧💧💧💧💧💧💧	Water 💧💧💧💧💧💧💧💧		Water 💧💧💧💧💧💧💧

Week of _____

Keep your lives free from the love of money and be content with what you have, because God has said, "Never will I leave you; never will I forsake you."

Hebrews 13:5

Prayer Request

PERSONAL REQUEST: _____

_____

_____

_____

_____

FAMILY REQUEST: _____

_____

_____

_____

_____

_____

PROFESSIONAL REQUEST: _____

_____

_____

_____

_____

_____

_____

Goals

PERSONAL GOALS: _____

_____

_____

_____

_____

_____

_____

FAMILY GOALS: _____

_____

_____

_____

_____

_____

PROFESSIONAL GOALS: _____

_____

_____

_____

_____

_____

Important Dates:

Event Name_____

Date_____

Event Name_____

Date_____

Event Name_____

Date_____

Mind and Body

- Do remember to call someone you love.
- Do remember to exercise your mind and body.
- Do remember to drink plenty of water
- Do remember to get plenty of rest.

Week of _____

	Monday	Tuesday	Wednesday
5 am			
6 am			
7 am			
8 am			
9 am			
10 am			
11 am			
12 pm			
1 pm			
2 pm			
3 pm			
4 pm			
5 pm			
6 pm			
7 pm			
8 pm			
9 pm			
10 pm			
	Water ◊◊◊◊◊◊◊◊	Water ◊◊◊◊◊◊◊◊	Water ◊◊◊◊◊◊◊◊

	Thursday	Friday		Saturday
5 am			9 am	
6 am			10 am	
7 am			11 am	
8 am			12 pm	
9 am			1 pm	
10 am			2 pm	
11 am			3 pm	
12 pm			4 pm	
1 pm				Water 💧💧💧💧💧💧💧
2 pm				Sunday
3 pm			9 am	
4 pm			10 am	
5 pm			11 am	
6 pm			12 pm	
7 pm			1 pm	
8 pm			2 pm	
9 pm			3 pm	
10 pm			4 pm	
	Water 💧💧💧💧💧💧💧	Water 💧💧💧💧💧💧💧		Water 💧💧💧💧💧💧💧

Week of _____

> If only you had paid attention to my commands, your peace would have been like a river, your well-being like the waves of the sea.
>
> Isaiah 48:18

Prayer Request

PERSONAL REQUEST: _____

_____

_____

_____

_____

FAMILY REQUEST: _____

_____

_____

_____

_____

_____

PROFESSIONAL REQUEST: _____

_____

_____

_____

_____

_____

_____

Goals

PERSONAL GOALS: _____

_____

_____

_____

_____

_____

_____

FAMILY GOALS: _____

_____

_____

_____

_____

_____

PROFESSIONAL GOALS: _____

_____

_____

_____

_____

_____

Important Dates:

Event Name_____

Date_____

Event Name_____

Date_____

Event Name_____

Date_____

Mind and Body

- Do remember to call someone you love.
- Do remember to exercise your mind and body.
- Do remember to drink plenty of water
- Do remember to get plenty of rest.

Week of _____

	Monday	Tuesday	Wednesday
5 am			
6 am			
7 am			
8 am			
9 am			
10 am			
11 am			
12 pm			
1 pm			
2 pm			
3 pm			
4 pm			
5 pm			
6 pm			
7 pm			
8 pm			
9 pm			
10 pm			
	Water 💧💧💧💧💧💧💧💧	Water 💧💧💧💧💧💧💧💧	Water 💧💧💧💧💧💧💧💧

	Thursday	Friday		Saturday
5 am			9 am	
6 am			10 am	
7 am			11 am	
8 am			12 pm	
9 am			1 pm	
10 am			2 pm	
11 am			3 pm	
12 pm			4 pm	
1 pm				Water 🌢🌢🌢🌢🌢🌢🌢
2 pm				Sunday
3 pm			9 am	
4 pm			10 am	
5 pm			11 am	
6 pm			12 pm	
7 pm			1 pm	
8 pm			2 pm	
9 pm			3 pm	
10 pm			4 pm	
	Water 🌢🌢🌢🌢🌢🌢🌢🌢	Water 🌢🌢🌢🌢🌢🌢🌢🌢		Water 🌢🌢🌢🌢🌢🌢🌢

Week of _____

Say to him: 'Long life to you! Good health to you and your household! And good health to all that is yours!

1 Samuel 25:6

Prayer Request

PERSONAL REQUEST: _____

_____

_____

_____

_____

FAMILY REQUEST: _____

_____

_____

_____

_____

_____

PROFESSIONAL REQUEST: _____

_____

_____

_____

_____

_____

_____

Goals

PERSONAL GOALS: _____

_____

_____

_____

_____

_____

_____

FAMILY GOALS: _____

_____

_____

_____

_____

_____

PROFESSIONAL GOALS: _____

_____

_____

_____

_____

_____

Important Dates:

Event Name_____

Date_____

Event Name_____

Date_____

Event Name_____

Date_____

Mind and Body

- Do remember to call someone you love.
- Do remember to exercise your mind and body.
- Do remember to drink plenty of water
- Do remember to get plenty of rest.

Week of _____

	Monday	Tuesday	Wednesday
5 am			
6 am			
7 am			
8 am			
9 am			
10 am			
11 am			
12 pm			
1 pm			
2 pm			
3 pm			
4 pm			
5 pm			
6 pm			
7 pm			
8 pm			
9 pm			
10 pm			
	Water ◊◊◊◊◊◊◊◊	Water ◊◊◊◊◊◊◊◊	Water ◊◊◊◊◊◊◊◊

	Thursday	Friday		Saturday
5 am			9 am	
6 am			10 am	
7 am			11 am	
8 am			12 pm	
9 am			1 pm	
10 am			2 pm	
11 am			3 pm	
12 pm			4 pm	
1 pm				Water ◊◊◊◊◊◊◊◊
2 pm				Sunday
3 pm			9 am	
4 pm			10 am	
5 pm			11 am	
6 pm			12 pm	
7 pm			1 pm	
8 pm			2 pm	
9 pm			3 pm	
10 pm			4 pm	
	Water ◊◊◊◊◊◊◊◊	Water ◊◊◊◊◊◊◊◊		Water ◊◊◊◊◊◊◊

Week of _____

My command is this: Love each other as I have loved you.

John 15:12

Prayer Request

PERSONAL REQUEST: _____

_____

_____

_____

_____

FAMILY REQUEST: _____

_____

_____

_____

_____

_____

PROFESSIONAL REQUEST: _____

_____

_____

_____

_____

_____

_____

Goals

PERSONAL GOALS: _____

_____

_____

_____

_____

_____

_____

FAMILY GOALS: _____

_____

_____

_____

_____

_____

PROFESSIONAL GOALS: _____

_____

_____

_____

_____

_____

Important Dates:

Event Name_____

Date_____

Event Name_____

Date_____

Event Name_____

Date_____

Mind and Body

- Do remember to call someone you love.
- Do remember to exercise your mind and body.
- Do remember to drink plenty of water
- Do remember to get plenty of rest.

Week of _____

	Monday	Tuesday	Wednesday
5 am			
6 am			
7 am			
8 am			
9 am			
10 am			
11 am			
12 pm			
1 pm			
2 pm			
3 pm			
4 pm			
5 pm			
6 pm			
7 pm			
8 pm			
9 pm			
10 pm			
	Water ８ drops	Water ８ drops	Water ８ drops

	Thursday	Friday		Saturday
5 am			9 am	
6 am			10 am	
7 am			11 am	
8 am			12 pm	
9 am			1 pm	
10 am			2 pm	
11 am			3 pm	
12 pm			4 pm	
1 pm				Water 💧💧💧💧💧💧💧
2 pm				Sunday
3 pm			9 am	
4 pm			10 am	
5 pm			11 am	
6 pm			12 pm	
7 pm			1 pm	
8 pm			2 pm	
9 pm			3 pm	
10 pm			4 pm	
	Water 💧💧💧💧💧💧💧💧	Water 💧💧💧💧💧💧💧💧		Water 💧💧💧💧💧💧💧

Week of _____

He and all his family were devout and God-fearing; he gave generously to those in need and prayed to God regularly.

Acts 10:2

Prayer Request

PERSONAL REQUEST: _____

_____

_____

_____

_____

FAMILY REQUEST: _____

_____

_____

_____

_____

_____

PROFESSIONAL REQUEST: _____

_____

_____

_____

_____

_____

_____

Goals

PERSONAL GOALS: _____

_____

_____

_____

_____

_____

_____

FAMILY GOALS: _____

_____

_____

_____

_____

_____

PROFESSIONAL GOALS: _____

_____

_____

_____

_____

_____

Important Dates:

Event Name_____

Date_____

Event Name_____

Date_____

Event Name_____

Date_____

Mind and Body

- Do remember to call someone you love.
- Do remember to exercise your mind and body.
- Do remember to drink plenty of water
- Do remember to get plenty of rest.

Week of _____

	Monday	Tuesday	Wednesday
5 am			
6 am			
7 am			
8 am			
9 am			
10 am			
11 am			
12 pm			
1 pm			
2 pm			
3 pm			
4 pm			
5 pm			
6 pm			
7 pm			
8 pm			
9 pm			
10 pm			
	Water 💧💧💧💧💧💧💧💧	Water 💧💧💧💧💧💧💧💧	Water 💧💧💧💧💧💧💧💧

	Thursday	Friday		Saturday
5 am			9 am	
6 am			10 am	
7 am			11 am	
8 am			12 pm	
9 am			1 pm	
10 am			2 pm	
11 am			3 pm	
12 pm			4 pm	
1 pm				Water 💧💧💧💧💧💧💧
2 pm				Sunday
3 pm			9 am	
4 pm			10 am	
5 pm			11 am	
6 pm			12 pm	
7 pm			1 pm	
8 pm			2 pm	
9 pm			3 pm	
10 pm			4 pm	
	Water 💧💧💧💧💧💧💧	Water 💧💧💧💧💧💧💧		Water 💧💧💧💧💧💧💧

Week of _____

"Come to me, all you who are weary and burdened, and I will give you rest. Take my yoke upon you and learn from me, for I am gentle and humble in heart, and you will find rest for your souls. For my yoke is easy and my burden is light."

Matthew 11:28-30

Prayer Request

PERSONAL REQUEST: _____

_____

_____

_____

_____

FAMILY REQUEST: _____

_____

_____

_____

_____

_____

PROFESSIONAL REQUEST: _____

_____

_____

_____

_____

_____

_____

Goals

PERSONAL GOALS: _____

_____

_____

_____

_____

_____

_____

FAMILY GOALS: _____

_____

_____

_____

_____

_____

PROFESSIONAL GOALS: _____

_____

_____

_____

_____

_____

_____

Important Dates:

Event Name_____

Date_____

Event Name_____

Date_____

Event Name_____

Date_____

Mind and Body

- Do remember to call someone you love.
- Do remember to exercise your mind and body.
- Do remember to drink plenty of water
- Do remember to get plenty of rest.

Week of _____

	Monday	Tuesday	Wednesday
5 am			
6 am			
7 am			
8 am			
9 am			
10 am			
11 am			
12 pm			
1 pm			
2 pm			
3 pm			
4 pm			
5 pm			
6 pm			
7 pm			
8 pm			
9 pm			
10 pm			
	Water ὁὁὁὁὁὁὁὁ	Water ὁὁὁὁὁὁὁὁ	Water ὁὁὁὁὁὁὁὁ

	Thursday	Friday		Saturday
5 am			9 am	
6 am			10 am	
7 am			11 am	
8 am			12 pm	
9 am			1 pm	
10 am			2 pm	
11 am			3 pm	
12 pm			4 pm	
1 pm				Water 〇〇〇〇〇〇〇〇
2 pm				Sunday
3 pm			9 am	
4 pm			10 am	
5 pm			11 am	
6 pm			12 pm	
7 pm			1 pm	
8 pm			2 pm	
9 pm			3 pm	
10 pm			4 pm	
	Water 〇〇〇〇〇〇〇〇	Water 〇〇〇〇〇〇〇〇		Water 〇〇〇〇〇〇〇〇

Week of _____

> But when he, the Spirit of truth, comes, he will guide you into all the truth. He will not speak on his own; he will speak only what he hears, and he will tell you what is yet to come.
>
> John 16:13

Prayer Request

PERSONAL REQUEST: _____

_____

_____

_____

_____

FAMILY REQUEST: _____

_____

_____

_____

_____

_____

PROFESSIONAL REQUEST: _____

_____

_____

_____

_____

_____

_____

Goals

PERSONAL GOALS: _____

_____

_____

_____

_____

_____

_____

FAMILY GOALS: _____

_____

_____

_____

_____

_____

PROFESSIONAL GOALS: _____

_____

_____

_____

_____

_____

Important Dates:

Event Name_____

Date_____

Event Name_____

Date_____

Event Name_____

Date_____

Mind and Body

- Do remember to call someone you love.
- Do remember to exercise your mind and body.
- Do remember to drink plenty of water
- Do remember to get plenty of rest.

Week of _____

	Monday	Tuesday	Wednesday
5 am			
6 am			
7 am			
8 am			
9 am			
10 am			
11 am			
12 pm			
1 pm			
2 pm			
3 pm			
4 pm			
5 pm			
6 pm			
7 pm			
8 pm			
9 pm			
10 pm			
	Water ◊◊◊◊◊◊◊◊	Water ◊◊◊◊◊◊◊◊	Water ◊◊◊◊◊◊◊◊

	Thursday	Friday		Saturday
5 am			9 am	
6 am			10 am	
7 am			11 am	
8 am			12 pm	
9 am			1 pm	
10 am			2 pm	
11 am			3 pm	
12 pm			4 pm	
1 pm				Water 💧💧💧💧💧💧💧
2 pm				**Sunday**
3 pm			9 am	
4 pm			10 am	
5 pm			11 am	
6 pm			12 pm	
7 pm			1 pm	
8 pm			2 pm	
9 pm			3 pm	
10 pm			4 pm	
	Water 💧💧💧💧💧💧💧	Water 💧💧💧💧💧💧💧		Water 💧💧💧💧💧💧💧

Week of _____

Cast all your anxiety on him because he cares for you.

1 Peter 5:7

Prayer Request

PERSONAL REQUEST: _____

_____

_____

_____

_____

FAMILY REQUEST: _____

_____

_____

_____

_____

_____

PROFESSIONAL REQUEST: _____

_____

_____

_____

_____

_____

_____

Goals

PERSONAL GOALS: _____

_____

_____

_____

_____

_____

_____

FAMILY GOALS: _____

_____

_____

_____

_____

_____

PROFESSIONAL GOALS: _____

_____

_____

_____

_____

_____

_____

Important Dates:

Event Name_____

Date_____

Event Name_____

Date_____

Event Name_____

Date_____

Mind and Body

- Do remember to call someone you love.
- Do remember to exercise your mind and body.
- Do remember to drink plenty of water
- Do remember to get plenty of rest.

Week of _____

	Monday	Tuesday	Wednesday
5 am			
6 am			
7 am			
8 am			
9 am			
10 am			
11 am			
12 pm			
1 pm			
2 pm			
3 pm			
4 pm			
5 pm			
6 pm			
7 pm			
8 pm			
9 pm			
10 pm			
	Water ◊◊◊◊◊◊◊◊	Water ◊◊◊◊◊◊◊◊	Water ◊◊◊◊◊◊◊◊

	Thursday	Friday		Saturday
5 am			9 am	
6 am			10 am	
7 am			11 am	
8 am			12 pm	
9 am			1 pm	
10 am			2 pm	
11 am			3 pm	
12 pm			4 pm	
1 pm				Water ◊◊◊◊◊◊◊◊
2 pm				Sunday
3 pm			9 am	
4 pm			10 am	
5 pm			11 am	
6 pm			12 pm	
7 pm			1 pm	
8 pm			2 pm	
9 pm			3 pm	
10 pm			4 pm	
	Water ◊◊◊◊◊◊◊◊	Water ◊◊◊◊◊◊◊◊		Water ◊◊◊◊◊◊◊◊

Week of _____

My times are in your hands; deliver me from the hands of my enemies, from those who pursue me.

Psalm 31:15

Prayer Request

PERSONAL REQUEST: _____

_____

_____

_____

_____

FAMILY REQUEST: _____

_____

_____

_____

_____

PROFESSIONAL REQUEST: _____

_____

_____

_____

_____

_____

Goals

PERSONAL GOALS: _____

_____

_____

_____

_____

_____

_____

FAMILY GOALS: _____

_____

_____

_____

_____

_____

PROFESSIONAL GOALS: _____

_____

_____

_____

_____

_____

_____

Important Dates:

Event Name_____

Date_____

Event Name_____

Date_____

Event Name_____

Date_____

Mind and Body

- Do remember to call someone you love.
- Do remember to exercise your mind and body.
- Do remember to drink plenty of water
- Do remember to get plenty of rest.

Week of _____

	Monday	Tuesday	Wednesday
5 am			
6 am			
7 am			
8 am			
9 am			
10 am			
11 am			
12 pm			
1 pm			
2 pm			
3 pm			
4 pm			
5 pm			
6 pm			
7 pm			
8 pm			
9 pm			
10 pm			
	Water ⬥⬥⬥⬥⬥⬥⬥⬥	Water ⬥⬥⬥⬥⬥⬥⬥⬥	Water ⬥⬥⬥⬥⬥⬥⬥⬥

	Thursday	Friday		Saturday
5 am			9 am	
6 am			10 am	
7 am			11 am	
8 am			12 pm	
9 am			1 pm	
10 am			2 pm	
11 am			3 pm	
12 pm			4 pm	
1 pm				Water ◊◊◊◊◊◊◊◊
2 pm				**Sunday**
3 pm			9 am	
4 pm			10 am	
5 pm			11 am	
6 pm			12 pm	
7 pm			1 pm	
8 pm			2 pm	
9 pm			3 pm	
10 pm			4 pm	
	Water ◊◊◊◊◊◊◊◊	Water ◊◊◊◊◊◊◊◊		Water ◊◊◊◊◊◊◊◊

Week of _____

So don't be afraid; you are worth more than many sparrows.

Matthew 10:31

Prayer Request

PERSONAL REQUEST: _____

_____

_____

_____

_____

FAMILY REQUEST: _____

_____

_____

_____

_____

_____

PROFESSIONAL REQUEST: _____

_____

_____

_____

_____

_____

_____

_____

Goals

PERSONAL GOALS: _____

_____

_____

_____

_____

_____

_____

FAMILY GOALS: _____

_____

_____

_____

_____

_____

PROFESSIONAL GOALS: _____

_____

_____

_____

_____

_____

Important Dates:

Event Name_____

Date_____

Event Name_____

Date_____

Event Name_____

Date_____

Mind and Body

- Do remember to call someone you love.
- Do remember to exercise your mind and body.
- Do remember to drink plenty of water
- Do remember to get plenty of rest.

Week of _____

	Monday	Tuesday	Wednesday
5 am			
6 am			
7 am			
8 am			
9 am			
10 am			
11 am			
12 pm			
1 pm			
2 pm			
3 pm			
4 pm			
5 pm			
6 pm			
7 pm			
8 pm			
9 pm			
10 pm			
	Water ⧫⧫⧫⧫⧫⧫⧫⧫	Water ⧫⧫⧫⧫⧫⧫⧫⧫	Water ⧫⧫⧫⧫⧫⧫⧫⧫

	Thursday	Friday		Saturday
5 am			9 am	
6 am			10 am	
7 am			11 am	
8 am			12 pm	
9 am			1 pm	
10 am			2 pm	
11 am			3 pm	
12 pm			4 pm	
1 pm				Water ◊◊◊◊◊◊◊
2 pm				Sunday
3 pm			9 am	
4 pm			10 am	
5 pm			11 am	
6 pm			12 pm	
7 pm			1 pm	
8 pm			2 pm	
9 pm			3 pm	
10 pm			4 pm	
	Water ◊◊◊◊◊◊◊	Water ◊◊◊◊◊◊◊		Water ◊◊◊◊◊◊◊

Week of _____

A heart at peace gives life to the body, but envy rots the bones.

Proverbs 14:30

Prayer Request

PERSONAL REQUEST: _____

_____

_____

_____

_____

FAMILY REQUEST: _____

_____

_____

_____

_____

_____

PROFESSIONAL REQUEST: _____

_____

_____

_____

_____

_____

_____

Goals

PERSONAL GOALS: _____

_____

_____

_____

_____

_____

_____

FAMILY GOALS: _____

_____

_____

_____

_____

_____

PROFESSIONAL GOALS: _____

_____

_____

_____

_____

_____

Important Dates:

Event Name_____

Date_____

Event Name_____

Date_____

Event Name_____

Date_____

Mind and Body

- Do remember to call someone you love.
- Do remember to exercise your mind and body.
- Do remember to drink plenty of water
- Do remember to get plenty of rest.

Week of _____

	Monday	Tuesday	Wednesday
5 am			
6 am			
7 am			
8 am			
9 am			
10 am			
11 am			
12 pm			
1 pm			
2 pm			
3 pm			
4 pm			
5 pm			
6 pm			
7 pm			
8 pm			
9 pm			
10 pm			
	Water ◊◊◊◊◊◊◊◊	Water ◊◊◊◊◊◊◊◊	Water ◊◊◊◊◊◊◊◊

	Thursday	Friday		Saturday
5 am			9 am	
6 am			10 am	
7 am			11 am	
8 am			12 pm	
9 am			1 pm	
10 am			2 pm	
11 am			3 pm	
12 pm			4 pm	
1 pm				Water 💧💧💧💧💧💧💧💧
2 pm				Sunday
3 pm			9 am	
4 pm			10 am	
5 pm			11 am	
6 pm			12 pm	
7 pm			1 pm	
8 pm			2 pm	
9 pm			3 pm	
10 pm			4 pm	
	Water 💧💧💧💧💧💧💧💧	Water 💧💧💧💧💧💧💧💧		Water 💧💧💧💧💧💧💧💧

Week of _____

If either of them falls down, one can help the other up. But pity anyone who falls and has no one to help them up.

Ecclesiastes 4:10

Prayer Request

PERSONAL REQUEST: _____

_____

_____

_____

_____

FAMILY REQUEST: _____

_____

_____

_____

_____

_____

PROFESSIONAL REQUEST: _____

_____

_____

_____

_____

_____

_____

Goals

PERSONAL GOALS: _____

_____

_____

_____

_____

_____

_____

FAMILY GOALS: _____

_____

_____

_____

_____

_____

_____

PROFESSIONAL GOALS: _____

_____

_____

_____

_____

_____

_____

Important Dates:

Event Name_____

Date_____

Event Name_____

Date_____

Event Name_____

Date_____

Mind and Body

- Do remember to call someone you love.
- Do remember to exercise your mind and body.
- Do remember to drink plenty of water
- Do remember to get plenty of rest.

Week of _____

	Monday	Tuesday	Wednesday
5 am			
6 am			
7 am			
8 am			
9 am			
10 am			
11 am			
12 pm			
1 pm			
2 pm			
3 pm			
4 pm			
5 pm			
6 pm			
7 pm			
8 pm			
9 pm			
10 pm			
	Water ὄὄὄὄὄὄὄὄ	Water ὄὄὄὄὄὄὄὄ	Water ὄὄὄὄὄὄὄὄ

	Thursday	Friday		Saturday
5 am			9 am	
6 am			10 am	
7 am			11 am	
8 am			12 pm	
9 am			1 pm	
10 am			2 pm	
11 am			3 pm	
12 pm			4 pm	
1 pm				Water 💧💧💧💧💧💧💧
2 pm				Sunday
3 pm			9 am	
4 pm			10 am	
5 pm			11 am	
6 pm			12 pm	
7 pm			1 pm	
8 pm			2 pm	
9 pm			3 pm	
10 pm			4 pm	
	Water 💧💧💧💧💧💧💧💧	Water 💧💧💧💧💧💧💧💧		Water 💧💧💧💧💧💧💧

Week of _____

She watches over the affairs of her household and does not eat the bread of idleness.

Proverbs 31:27

Prayer Request

PERSONAL REQUEST: _____

_____

_____

_____

_____

FAMILY REQUEST: _____

_____

_____

_____

_____

_____

PROFESSIONAL REQUEST: _____

_____

_____

_____

_____

_____

_____

Goals

PERSONAL GOALS: _____

_____

_____

_____

_____

_____

_____

_____

FAMILY GOALS: _____

_____

_____

_____

_____

_____

_____

PROFESSIONAL GOALS: _____

_____

_____

_____

_____

_____

_____

Important Dates:

Event Name_____

Date_____

Event Name_____

Date_____

Event Name_____

Date_____

Mind and Body

- Do remember to call someone you love.
- Do remember to exercise your mind and body.
- Do remember to drink plenty of water
- Do remember to get plenty of rest.

Week of _____

	Monday	Tuesday	Wednesday
5 am			
6 am			
7 am			
8 am			
9 am			
10 am			
11 am			
12 pm			
1 pm			
2 pm			
3 pm			
4 pm			
5 pm			
6 pm			
7 pm			
8 pm			
9 pm			
10 pm			
	Water ♢♢♢♢♢♢♢♢	Water ♢♢♢♢♢♢♢♢	Water ♢♢♢♢♢♢♢♢

	Thursday	Friday		Saturday
5 am			9 am	
6 am			10 am	
7 am			11 am	
8 am			12 pm	
9 am			1 pm	
10 am			2 pm	
11 am			3 pm	
12 pm			4 pm	
1 pm				Water 🜄🜄🜄🜄🜄🜄🜄
2 pm				Sunday
3 pm			9 am	
4 pm			10 am	
5 pm			11 am	
6 pm			12 pm	
7 pm			1 pm	
8 pm			2 pm	
9 pm			3 pm	
10 pm			4 pm	
	Water 🜄🜄🜄🜄🜄🜄🜄🜄	Water 🜄🜄🜄🜄🜄🜄🜄🜄		Water 🜄🜄🜄🜄🜄🜄🜄

Year-End Reflections

Have you accomplished the goals you set forth?

___

What changes have your made that has helped you meet your goals?

___

If you haven't accomplished a goal, what stood in your way ?

___

What will you do to remove these obstacles for the future?

___

Blessings

But the plans of the Lord stand firm forever, the purposes of his heart through all generations.

Psalm 33:11

May the God of hope fill you with all joy and peace as you trust in him, so that you may overflow with hope by the power of the Holy Spirit.

Romans 15:13

The Lord within her is righteous; he does no wrong. Morning by morning he dispenses his justice, and every new day he does not fail, yet the unrighteous know no shame.

Zephaniah 3:5

To order next year's planner visit

www.womenontheriseny.com

Or email

info@womenontheriseny.com

www.ingramcontent.com/pod-product-compliance
Lightning Source LLC
Chambersburg PA
CBHW040327300426
44113CB00020B/2679